YOU
ARE
ENOUGH

ALSO BY PANACHE DESAI

Discovering Your Soul Signature:
A 33-Day Path to Purpose, Passion & Joy

YOU ARE ENOUGH

Revealing the Soul to Discover
Your Power, Potential, and Possibility

PANACHE DESAI

HarperOne
An Imprint of HarperCollinsPublishers

HarperOne

HarperCollins books may be purchased for educational, business, or sales promotional use. For information, please email the Special Markets Department at SPsales@harpercollins.com.

FIRST EDITION

Designed by Joy O'Meara

Library of Congress Cataloging-in-Publication Data is available upon request.

ISBN 978-0-06-293257-0

20 21 22 23 24   LSC   10 9 8 7 6 5 4 3 2 1

To my perfect reflection, my wife, Jan Desai.
Thank you for your love, patience, and unwavering belief in me.
This work is possible because of your generosity of spirit,
loving devotion, and dedication to the uplifting of all.

You are here to answer the call
to live your highest expression
and in doing so illuminate your life and the world.

—PANACHE DESAI

CONTENTS

YOU
ARE
ENOUGH

An Invitation

T DOESN'T MATTER HOW YOUR LIFE HAS UNFOLDED UP to this moment. I want you to remember this: *every single morning, you open your eyes and win the megamillion-dollar lottery of being alive.* With each second in the day, you are given 86,400 chances to choose differently than you have in the past. You are also given 28,800 breaths to act, think, and move from love. There is only ever one choice. Either you are living from your heart and moving toward your limitless potential, or you are continuing to live in fear and limitation.

When I entered this world and the doctors gave me that first slap, I had an appointed purpose to fulfill, *as we all do.* But as long as I resisted my design, as long as I tried to turn myself into something that I thought would be admired or loved by others, I could not fulfill it. It wasn't until I reached the depths of internal despair that I got in touch with the true reality that exists in and around us in every moment. In that surrender, I found the purpose, goodness, and connection that was my destiny.

Many traditions have a word for this experience: samadhi. Samadhi is the sacred remembrance of your Essential Self, which is one with God. It is knowing who you are, fully and authentically. It is an illumination, a recognition, a union. It is what we all crave at the deepest level of being. The desire for this union is that ceaseless internal hunger that keeps us searching *externally* for what paradoxically can only be found *internally.* I've seen this search in the thousands of people who come to me frightened, angry, sad, addicted, and abandoned. My message to those desperately seeking solutions outside of themselves is that the search begins and ends with you.

I am here to empower you to find your Essential Self and claim your peace. Most important, I'm here to ignite the remembrance that it already exists within you and help you become conscious of how a series of events and experiences have caused you to forget your own power, potential, light, and love.

At this point in the evolution of our species, I know samadhi is possible for everyone. Humanity is in the process of remembering; a collective awakening is being birthed in the world. And everything that is happening, politically, socially, environmentally—all the chaos—is there so that individuals can remember and realize their authentic Essential Selves. In the wake of widespread cacophony, pretenses and egoic structures are falling away, unveiling the true reality of love, kindness, and human connection. No longer is enlightenment reserved for monks, masters, and gurus. In fact, the more you try to replicate someone else's spiritual practice or journey, the further you find yourself from the power, beauty, and authenticity of who you truly are.

Samadhi is counterintuitive to your operating system, because it is not a matter of striving, grasping, or achieving. It isn't bestowed upon you based on the books you've read, the courses you've taken, or the influence of the spiritual path you've chosen to pursue. You don't need to renounce the physical world, live in an ashram, or meditate three times a day. You can have a beautiful family, enjoy a glass of wine, watch your favorite TV show, relax in a cozy home, and appreciate all the other gifts of this world.

To reach samadhi, all you truly need is yourself.

Your experience on this planet is as unique as one of the billions of stars in the clear indigo sky, and yet I believe you and I are on the same journey—one in which the Essential Self is emerging into conscious experience, shifting out of separation and suffering into connection and bliss. Rich or poor, married or single, employed or unemployed, young or old, male or female, Christian, Muslim, Hindu, Jew, or Buddhist, you are the soul coming to know the Essential Self as love.

Every single facet of your life contributes toward this greater evolution. The smiles that make your cheeks hurt. The continually griping employee or the controlling boss. The heartbreak that tries your very will to go on. Your children, siblings, parents, and grandparents. Even simple, mundane things—like a favorite sweater or the sliced banana you eat for breakfast. All the contrasting elements of your existence: the myriad of colors, textures, scenarios, agonies, ecstasies, and routines. There is a cosmic purpose for each aspect, which is that you, in your finite physical body, come to know your unbounded Divine Nature.

The Divine or God, as I define and have come to know it, is an infinite ocean of love that is the source of all experience, one that doesn't require anything from us—not even our belief in it. Any definition actually serves as a limitation. However, to give you a sign-post or to point toward infinity, the word "Divine" is the most expansive and least riddled with baggage. As you move through the book and encounter words like "God" or "Divine," know that I'm using them to continually point you back toward your limitless nature. Everything you experience, from your first precious breath until the moment you draw your last, supports you toward that end.

My intention in writing this book is to awaken you to the experience of the Divine Consciousness that is within you. I will help you accelerate your personal evolution, so that you will come to embody your limitless nature.

When you walk through this threshold, you will begin to experience life from the most expanded state possible—as though you are standing on a vast beach on the brink of sunrise, peaceful and serene. As the cobalt-black sky begins to fade, you know with certitude that you are not the darkness. Saturated purples, pinks, oranges, and yellows breach the horizon. The awe-inspiring palette of light and color climbs across the sky and stretches its arms toward you over the endless sea. It's coming to enfold you, to remind you. You are this light, and you are as powerful as the sun. Its radiance and purity are your divine birthright.

On those inevitable days when the clouds block your luminous nature, you will know that your Essential Self has not disappeared; it is only temporarily hidden from view. When violent thunderstorms arrive in your life, you will no longer be rocked from this solid foundation. No hurricane, earthquake, or tsunami will fool you into forgetting your Essential Nature.

Once you know yourself as the light, you will find that inner peace dominates every situation. It's not that you will never feel fear, anxiety, or anger, but you will no longer get lost in your pain. It will no longer drown out the light. You will clearly recognize it for what it is—a temporary cloud passing in the sky. When you understand this hidden dimension of your humanity, you can empower yourself to accelerate your evolution. In this acceleration, you will discover where you are now and examine how you got there; you will learn a new way of relating to this world and the process through which that new way is made manifest.

When you understand this hidden dimension of your humanity, you can empower yourself to accelerate your evolution.

A sacred universal energy permeates this book. This energy may act as a catalyst that stirs up old stories and beliefs, strong emotions, and physical, mental, and emotional wounds. Its purpose is to bring a lifetime of stored and blocked energy into harmony. There will be moments when you are overtaken by strong unresolved emotions and your tears will flow unchecked. Or you may even determine that none of this book's content has any relevance to your life—this is the most definitive red flag of them all. Persevere.

This book and the energy it transmits cannot dredge up anything that doesn't already exist within you. Cultivate the willingness and spaciousness to allow everything that you are experiencing physically, emotionally, spiritually, and psychologically to arise and enter your consciousness. This is the path of true spiritual awakening and ultimate self-realization. The stronger your reaction to what you are reading, the higher the likelihood that the content is exactly what you need to sit with as you move forward toward your redefinition. Each and every word plays a role in helping you reveal your highest Divine Nature.

In 2003, I received an awakening, a revelation as visceral as it was profound. My life up to that point had been one of varying degrees of powerful but fleeting spiritual encounters. I was born with the capacity to experience others' emotions and energy simply by being in proximity to them. While other four-year-old boys were busy watching their favorite cartoons, building forts, and fighting imaginary enemies like pirates and bank robbers, I was ensconced in a sacred atmosphere of prayer and worship for hours each day. At this tender age, I found great serenity in my grandmother's meditation room, the heart of her home. Amid the soft candlelight, gentle incense, and melodious echoes of her chanting, I was immersed in the sacred energy of a Presence beyond this world. What became woven within me was the most beautiful experience of profound peace, connection, and unconditional love, and it was this that would establish the remembrance deep within me of the messenger I was here to be.

My outer world could not have been more different. I grew up in East London in the late 1970s, a sprawling urban neighborhood that was anything but peaceful. It was a rowdy melting pot of nationalities, cultures, and strong beliefs and ideals, where people worked long and hard to provide the simplest of lives for their families. Pervading it all was a toughness that masked a mentality of fear, deprivation, and scarcity in an ever-evolving game of survival of the fittest. The dissonance between these two worlds would, for the first twenty years of my life, create an ever-increasing tug-of-war between my destiny and my need to fit in.

My unique gift for experiencing others' emotions and energy simply by being near them acted as a natural homing beacon to those who were stressed and careworn. Through some cosmic transference, internal blockages that were keeping their lives at a perceived disadvantage would dissolve in my presence. Family, friends, and complete strangers would go into heightened emotional states, crying or becoming very angry as they unburdened themselves to me. To a seven-year-old, these outbursts were always slightly bewildering and extremely unnerving. Their financial troubles, health scares, relationship challenges, and overwhelming feelings were beyond my years, but the overflow of raw emotion kept me rooted in my place.

I always felt responsible, wondering what I had done to cause all that emotion. I would tell my parents that some people just felt very, very heavy when they sat and talked with me. But after a period, these visitors would inevitably get up, and I would sense a "sparkliness" about them. And, in turn, their lives would dramatically shift in ways that made their day-to-day experiences seem almost miraculous. My energy would break loose the blocks or restrictions that limited them, shattering the walls they had created over decades, changing their energy and changing their lives.

While my family called it "a gift," this ability to sense a person's inner world was, to me, a growing nuisance that made me feel weird. And so I did what almost everyone on this planet does—I began to make choices that would help me feel more like everyone else.

Like most adolescents, I struggled to fit in at school, to find belonging with a group who might possibly have my back. My early spiritual immersion had opened a deep sensitivity within me that made relationships challenging. And so I floated. Not a jock, an intellectual, a rebel, or a druggie, I was an outlier, an easy target who was bullied. On good days I only got pushed around. On bad days I was beaten up. I learned how to adapt, using my empathic energy gift to read and match the intensity of any bully who got in my face. In that way, I became a worthy opponent. But with each choice to become something I wasn't, I paid a greater price. I was becoming inauthentic to my core.

As I struggled to claim my identity in my late teens, I chose to turn my back on the one thing that had created the strongest foundation for my being and my internal GPS, my grandma's spirituality. I found a new home in a thriving yet drug- and gang-infested underground music scene. As a popular MC, I established an enviable circle of acquaintants from all socioeconomic backgrounds— from London's heirs and heiresses to local celebrities to your regular Joes just trying to make it through another day. It gave me a false sense of respect and belonging, but did nothing to assuage the consuming loneliness I felt within.

When the time came to attend college, I made another choice that, although on the outside made my family proud, internally pushed me even further away from my authentic self. Rather than pursuing my lifelong passion, philosophy, I decided it was more important to make my grandfather proud and study law and business. Deep down I knew it wasn't for me, but a degree in philosophy wouldn't provide financial security or the respect of my grandfather through the lens of his Indian conditioning.

So, over the course of three years at the university, a growing sadness began to well up inside of me. I was paying the price for putting someone else's desires for my life before my own. I loved my grandfather and had great admiration for him. He had immigrated to London from India with three pounds to his name. Through old-fashioned hard work and dedication, he built an amazing life, enabling his wife and five children to join him.

He had become a success in his own right, and I felt compelled to validate his efforts and do something to carry them forward into a new generation. Society told me that there were certain tried and true ways to do that, so I set out to follow them diligently. I was the oldest grandchild. I wanted to make him proud. I believed I was prepared to carry the mantle of the Desai legacy into the next generation. But in conforming to an external ideal of success, I lost sight of my own purpose, my reason for being.

There are moments in each of our lives when something greater—something incontrovertible—steps in to help us realign with our truest lives and most authentic selves. This *perceived* crisis or trauma either shakes our world to its core or tears everything apart so that we are launched once again in the direction of our best lives, the most authentic expression of who we are each here to be.

I had experienced all that a young man could want from the world, and I was still empty and miserable. My loneliness and the ever-increasing pain of living a life that was spiraling out of control was suffocating. And then, in the very early hours of a Saturday morning I will never forget, I came face-to-face with how precious life is and how in an instant everything can change forever.

I had been MCing and was ready to once again party into the night. As I neared the bar to order a drink, I was jumped by three drunks. Yelling racial slurs, they threw me to the ground and began kicking and punching me. Luckily, the bouncers at the club knew me and saw what was happening. They broke up the fight and dragged me to my feet. Badly shaken, cut, and with a bruised body and ego, I was still unwilling to head home. I simply couldn't face my parents, so I went to yet another after-hours club. Once inside, I was confronted with another fight. This time guns were involved. Soon the place was surrounded by the police. As in a hostage situation, everyone in the bar was individually escorted from the club.

Life's events were escalating in intensity in order to wake me up. Choice after choice throughout my early adulthood had been made from a place of needing to fit in, wanting to belong. Each step took me further away from my happiness, my inner connection. The whispers at first were faint. This final experience was the two-by-four across the head. I needed no further message from the cosmos. My life changed permanently from that point on. I headed home, both literally and figuratively. It was time to rediscover the spirituality of my childhood. Within days I had packed my bags and gone off to enter an ashram and reconnect with the truth of who I was.

I will always remember that gut-wrenching conversation with my mother before I left. It was as though I had stepped through a looking glass and gone back to being a child who had been caught doing something that was strictly forbidden. I grasped her hands in mine. I needed to feel her presence, I needed to sense her energy, as I whispered that I had to leave. The words gained intoxicating speed as I rushed to explain that the greater forces of life had grabbed me by the shoulders and shaken me to my very core. The life choices that I had been making were so out of alignment with my innermost self that I was living a giant lie. It was the hardest conversation I'd ever had, and yet she met my words with love, understanding, and spaciousness. Her steadfast belief in things unfolding in some greater natural order allowed me to let go of my own harsh criticism.

The sincere longing to rediscover the truth of who I was here to be was my only companion during my long and sleepless transatlantic flight. As I tentatively entered the sacred space at the ashram for the first time, the sounds of the mantras, the heavy smell of incense, and the warm welcome of loving devotees offering their selfless service touched a deep remembering within me. I shaved my head, lived austerely, offered selfless service, and meditated for long hours each day. I never looked back. I was home.

After six months I returned to London to pack my bags for good. I knew my future lay somewhere in the United States.

I decided to travel cross-country and see if the West Coast felt more in alignment. I was patient with myself, nonjudgmental, and open to the people I met and the places I visited along the way. And with time, I came to discover my destiny and experience a profound sense of self-awareness, passion, and purpose.

The unusual gift that was as much a part of me as my fingerprints and brown eyes intensified as I headed west. In retrospect, I can see that I was in an extended period of preparation. As my own personal energy frequency was being expanded, I began to experience everything that was out of alignment with my Essential Self.

Within days of arriving in Los Angeles, I found an apartment. I quickly began meeting people who were also on the search for inner integrity. And yet, as much as I had a physical address, I had yet to fully arrive. I was open and curious and was being moved around like a chess piece from one spiritual teacher to another. They all had the same message for me: I was here to facilitate an awakening; I had come to support the consciousness of the world. And yet I was frustrated deeply, because I couldn't see how someone as flawed as me could be the choice for this kind of responsibility. I couldn't own it for myself.

My frustration grew and grew. And then one day, on the cusp of 2003, I did the unthinkable. I "called out" the Divine. In anger I shouted unbelievable demands: "If you're here I need to see you! If you exist, I need to feel you! If I'm here to be a messenger, if I'm truly here to do something on your behalf, than I have to experience who or what you are."

I'll never forget what happened next. As the stroke of midnight neared on New Year's Eve, I was sitting in my small apartment when I suddenly felt as if the room was filled with beings I couldn't see. I knew that I was no longer alone. The initial fear melted into a level of profound peace and connection I had known only fleetingly before. It lulled me into a deeply relaxed state of being, so that I could be open for what was to come. My eyes were closed, and yet suddenly I was bathed in brilliant light and intense energy. My body began to shake with wild tremors. At first, I felt terrified, unable to breathe, but a part of me knew that it was imperative to try and relax into this current of extreme energy in order to not be crushed by it.

For a moment I actually thought I was having a massive heart attack. Once again, I yelled out in fear that this intensity was too much. Wave after wave of emotion was moving through me. I was forced into surrender, and the only thing I could do in each moment was to give myself over to the discomfort, pain, and trauma that was moving up and out of my body.

Time had no meaning. I was suspended in a state of perpetual expansion. Throughout the entire night and into the early morning, the force moved through me and surrounded me simultaneously. It was all-encompassing, all-embracing. An ocean of infinite energy—love in its most transcendent form. The potential of life in its most expansive nature. Words do not exist that can describe what I saw, felt, and experienced. This was an encounter of divine union.

When I awoke the next morning, absolutely everything that I had taken for granted had a breathtaking luminosity about it. My toothbrush, my jeans, the car keys, the door handle. Even the garbage blown into the alleyways and the homeless who used it to cushion their bodies not only emitted light, but pulsed with love. My heart had merged with the heart of the Divine, which allowed me to perceive everything at a level of vibration and frequency. I was now seeing and feeling without judgment or fear. Everything had softened. This luminosity filled my days with endless wonder.

The experience of my awakening had completely shifted my outer focus to an inner one, in which I no longer looked to the world to deliver joy, love, or belonging. My happiness was no longer based on the approval of others. I was in a state of self-generated bliss and peace. Time had no meaning.

The shifts I experienced within also attracted people in my community. As friends began to hear about my experience, they were excited to pass it on to others.

Within weeks, people were knocking on my door and filling my apartment. They simply wanted to sit with me. They longed to feel what there was to feel. And yet I was clear; I was not here to be anyone's guru.

It took more than three months, but eventually the intensity of the experience *seemed* to ease—in reality, it had just become my natural state. The gift I had as a child magnified, as did the understanding that I was only a vector for this energy, not its source.

Years later, the day came once again when I knew it was time to let go of the life I had built on the West Coast and move on. I awoke one morning and simply knew that my work was done. This chapter was complete. I was once again being moved by a force that was greater than my own will, and my only job was to trust. It was instinctual, and like the geese that migrated over my childhood London home as the days grew shorter and the temperature grew colder, I packed my bags and instinctually headed east.

Yes, I was sad. Once again, I was leaving behind everything that I had come to know and love. But little did I perceive that the heartbreak of lost relationships and the need to expand my awareness and teachings were the universe's way of placing me in the direct path of meeting the beautiful, wise, and powerful woman who would become my business partner and wife and mother to our four children.

I know this: there is an opening in every perceived difficulty through which the majesty of the Divine seeps into our existence. No experience in life, however painful, is ever wasted.

During the years following that initial revelation that I was here to be a messenger of awakening and divine love, I slowly integrated it into my life as a constant. It is now fully a part of me. No pleasure in this world can match how I feel inside—no white-sand beach, million-dollar check, or lofty position on a global stage. There is internal wholeness, nothing to be added or taken away.

The meaning I had sought, the peace and fulfillment I had been told were possible had revealed themselves within my being. My struggles, my fears, my resistance, and my unworthiness ended and had been replaced by a permanent peace, bliss, joy, and contentment.

Throughout my life, every choice, every experience, every challenge, and every celebration has woven itself into the tapestry of the stories I tell and the passion and possibility I share with people from across this globe to uncover their Essential Self and live their limitless lives.

Revealing your Essential Self is a process of coming into harmony and alignment with your soul, which requires that you accept and embrace all that you are—every quality, every nuance, every experience, every perceived mistake, everything you see as bad, ugly, divisive, and destructive. I understand that this may sound beyond what you think you are capable of. It might feel like pressing upon a throbbing subdermal infection, hot and painful to the slightest touch.

Or maybe you are so dissociated from your internal conflicts that you do not even know where to start. I've heard every excuse for why this journey may seem too overwhelming to even begin. "But, Panache, you don't know what I've done." "You can't imagine whom I've hurt." You don't know the sins I've committed." "You'd walk away from me if you realized the magnitude of my mistakes."

As much as these statements may seem convincing or even true to you, they can never invalidate the ultimate truth: you are loved by God exactly as you are. Right now. In this moment.

The commitment of this journey is your willingness to meet yourself with love and acceptance, here and now.

The great inventor Nikola Tesla once said, "When you want to know the secrets of the universe, think in terms of energy, frequency, vibration." He understood that we are vibrational beings living in a vibrational universe. This means that anything you are running from, denying, or suppressing is simply a form of energy. Some energies are denser or of lower frequency. Some are lighter and more expansive. But it is all just energy. Nothing more, nothing less.

Perhaps your greatest obstacle to fulfillment is all the ways you have been conditioned to label, judge, and categorize those energies. You spend great stretches of time in your life running from "demons" you believe would eat you alive if you ever stopped and dared to face them. But it is your refusal to deal with them that is eating you alive.

My intention is to inspire you to have the courage to approach those energies wholeheartedly, with radical self-love and acceptance, so that you can relax in the face of them and simultaneously raise your frequency to the point where they naturally slough out of your reality. Through this process you will move from a platform of fear to a platform of love. It has worked for many. It can work for you.

When you dare to turn your attention inward, you can come into coherence with your highest frequency, simultaneously relinquishing all you are not. You undergo an accelerated self-realization through which you surrender the defenses of your ego, because you no longer have need of them to survive. Your life takes on fresh vitality as your heart opens wide, and you feel as though you have finally made it home.

Samadhi is a fundamental realignment of energy that raises the frequency in which you reside. It is the union of the external with the core of your being, which is one with all life. Ultimately, it is knowing that you are nothing less than a spark of the Divine Light, which animates everyone and everything.

Right now, though, rather than looking within, you are continually trying to fit in and find your peace in the external environment. You embark on a spiritual path and then wait for some otherworldly experience to deliver enlightenment to your doorstep, as if it were a product you ordered online. You look to your parents, teachers, society, religion, spiritual practice, or that lovely little fairy godmother to come and give you a badge that says, "Welcome to the nirvana club."

But there is no true validation to be had that comes from without. *The very fact that you are breathing is your validation.*

There is absolutely nothing you can do, get, or accomplish that could make you any worthier of goodness than you are at this exact moment. Your place in the greater divine unfolding is enough. You are enough.

Take a deep breath and let that sink in. You are enough, exactly as you are.

The Divine constantly, wholly, and completely loves you and accepts you as you are. When you can fully accept that, you access your most natural state, which is peace.

> *There is absolutely nothing you can do, get, or accomplish that could make you any worthier of goodness than you are at this exact moment.*

Everything you have been told has been superimposed, layer after layer, circumstance after circumstance, year after year, over this peace that is your truth. Throughout your life you have had various bad experiences and emotional traumas, and each one has been imprinted in your energy field. Your evolutionary role is to peel back those layers and dissolve those imprints, not by analyzing them, rejecting them, or fighting against them, but by putting forth a consistent effort toward cultivating awareness, acceptance, and compassion for yourself.

Your Divine Essence has been with you all along, and it cannot wait for you to start on this journey of rediscovery. Through the energy of the words on these pages, you will be prompted to review the story of your life not through a lens of what you have achieved, milestones you have reached, or your perceived mistakes, but through the lens of your dear shining soul.

Know who you truly are. Know that joy is possible in all situations. Know that life can be exceptional, that you are exceptional. Know your own samadhi.

1

The Promise

THE WORLD—YOUR PARENTS, YOUR TEACHERS, your clan, your religion—made an agreement with you. It promised that if you live your life in the pursuit of certain milestones, if you grab the brass ring, if you achieve, you will be happy, healthy, wealthy, and wise. You will find fulfillment. You will gain love, respect, and honor. You will have "made it." You will be accepted. Worth will be bestowed upon you.

You are not even conscious that you made this agreement. Still, you have steadfastly followed the rules, like an obedient child in school, laces carefully tied in bunny-ear bows and No. 2 pencil in hand. You have strived to become someone whose life looks praiseworthy. It's been a dutiful performance, boxes neatly checked, *i*'s dotted, *t*'s crossed. You are a dedicated husband, a loving mother, a dependable friend, a solid employee. You've diligently held up your end of the bargain, but along the way you have forgotten who you once were.

You are not aware that you have lost touch with your authenticity; that you have covered over your true desires; that you have conformed to the expectations of others; that you have simply learned to "cope" in a world dominated by fear, limitation, scarcity, and ego. It's what your parents did, and it's what you see your peers doing. You have the job, the house, the car, the relationship, the family, the bank account, and the degrees. Or at least you grasped for it all, even if you weren't successful at getting it.

But now you feel disappointed, bewildered. The more you achieve and acquire, the more you feel like an empty vessel waiting to be filled up. You think, "Why do I feel this way? I've done the job. I've played by the rules and worked hard. Now where's the prize?"

*The more you achieve and acquire, the
more you feel like an empty vessel
waiting to be filled up.*

There is a growing sense of a letdown. What once started as a dull ache, hardly noticeable, has turned into a sharp pain that you can no longer ignore. Behind the scenes of the grand production that is life, you begin to realize that very few people are truly satisfied. They are searching for something just as you are. Has it all been a charade?

Whether you experience your separation from your Essential Self as a great emotional upheaval, a silent desperation, or a generalized feeling that life owes you something, the result is the same. A mind that runs in circles like a wild monkey in a cage. Seeking but never finding. Analyzing each letdown as an indicator of your unworthiness. Worrying about everything and nothing—while lying in bed at night, after dropping the kids off at school, on the train home from work. Meanwhile, you endlessly grab at satiation from the physical—food, sex, drugs, success, and material things—indiscriminately pushing away everything that doesn't fit into your "happiness" scenario.

You become at least slightly neurotic, desperate to ensure that your life reflects an enviable and immaculate image. This means keeping a rigid schedule, which staves off feelings of anxiety and panic, giving you the illusion of control. It means, perhaps, looking very busy all the time, but never really feeling that you are doing what matters. You may demand perfection in your immediate surroundings as a way to compensate for your inner emptiness: the silk throw pillows arranged on the white settee over the coordinating Oriental rug, the right organic food in your fridge, the art selected to impress, a closetful of designer shoes you've barely worn. Just looking at the shoes all lined up, so exquisite and beautiful, gives you a hit of "I am good enough."

And yet you have spent countless hours on your therapist's couch dealing with the assortment of addictions and attachments you've taken on as distractions. You discuss the same few issues dressed in different costumes, rehashing them over and over. Or maybe you've sought advice from a minister, rabbi, or guru, hoping that someone else can remove your obstacles for you. Still, on a rainy Sunday afternoon, curled up on your couch in your sweats, with no one around and nothing that needs your immediate attention, you feel it in your chest, a faint echo of something more. "Where is my peace? Where is my fulfillment? Where is my joy? They promised me everything, but now I feel disconnected, separate, and very much alone."

Perhaps suicide has crossed your mind. Perhaps you've endured a chronic illness, a failed marriage, or financial challenges. Or maybe you are not as far along in your filling of society's prescription for life. You've finished school, earned the degrees that made your parents happy, gotten a job that pays the bills, and found a partner who looks good on your arm. And yet there is a big colored section of your pie chart missing. You've been so attentive, so careful, so diligent. What could you have possibly overlooked in your compliant execution of happiness?

It has become clear that the promise is a lie. Even so, you're not quite ready to reject it—on some level it's all you have to believe in. And everyone else believes in it too. How is it possible that the majority could be so massively deceived? You are confused, but you also know in your heart of hearts that there is more, something right in front of you yet just beyond your grasp. You are floundering in your incompletion, hungry for truth. You have a vague inkling that peace, and maybe even something greater, is possible.

And you are right. The promise of genuine peace, joy,

and fulfillment is real, but the path to revealing it is un-expected and, to most, paradoxical. It will arise from within, once you return to authenticity. It will naturally emerge when you redefine what it means to be human and, most important, when you heal what I call your core wound—your perceived unworthiness.

The promise of genuine peace, joy, and fulfillment is real, but the path to revealing it is unexpected and, to most, paradoxical.

You see, your relationship to yourself is based on the role you have taken on in this life and other people's reactions to that role. But a role is not the real you. It is a mere facade—a foggy, manufactured version of your true, authentic brilliance. It is like a dim fluorescent light compared to the clean, bright rays of the sun. It is not "bad," but it is the source of limitation and discon-nection in your life. You've created this facade in search of fulfillment and belonging, but underneath it lies a powerful and grace-filled desire for connection, love, and oneness.

For the most part, your facade was formed over time through the medium of language—what has been spoken over you and what you have been conditioned to believe. That language, repeatedly delivered by parents, teachers, religion, and society, forms a vast intricate invisible construct—words that weave the script for the role you are to play in this lifetime: "You aren't smart enough." "You'll never amount to anything." "You're just not a natural people person." "You can't have those; they will make you fat."

Or more generally: "Only the strong survive." "Life is a struggle." "Things like that don't just happen for people like us." "Money doesn't grow on trees." "Behave well and you will go to heaven. Behave badly and you are going to hell."

Even phrases seemingly more benign: "You are such a sweet girl, quiet and respectful. You will make such a wonderful [fill in the blank]." "You are such a good boy, following all the rules. You will make a wonderful [fill in the blank]."

You have been meticulously conditioned over time through the unrelenting delivery of words like these. They have in part shaped and formed who you are today, how you think about things, and how you show up in the world. Every statement, every slight intonation, every parameter set for you is a different brick in your egoic structure, held together by the mortar of fear.

You continually maintain your facade, trying to make it more palatable to others. But inevitably a sense of unworthiness arises, because you are living out your life in separation from and ignorance of your true essence. You try to honor your parents, teachers, and society, and you want to trust and believe in what they told you. But something deep within rejects it. There is a sadness, an angst, a worry, a fear. Listen to and examine that restlessness, that subtle dissatisfaction. It is the awakening of transformation.

But transformation in the West has become about augmenting or improving the facade rather than freeing one from it. Not only has it become about bolstering self-regard, but it is also overly focused on the mind and body. Seldom is it focused on the soul—where the real power rests. The result is that when you try to hone a "spiritual" practice, you don't experience powerful shifts in your state of being and affairs. You meditate. You have a mantra. You do yoga. You attend spiritual courses. You spend three months at an ashram. You put in time, money, and effort to create transformation and gain a sense of fulfillment from who you are, only to come to realize that the work has amounted to an even more elaborate facade.

If you are at any point in time engaging in spiritual practice, it is for one of two reasons. Either you are intending to dissolve the created self—the false, fabricated, fear-based self that you've created over a lifetime out of the misdirected belief that you are not enough—and move closer to the soul and truth, or you are intending to bolster your ego in some way—to look cool, to be accepted and approved of, or to feel morally superior.

When your intention is to reveal your soul, you are consciously collapsing your facade, creating the possibility for genuine peace and fulfillment to emerge. To get there, you need to let go of the ego gratification you get from appearing "spiritual" or being known in some specific way that earns approval from your tribe or praise from society. You need to dig deep within yourself until you uncover your only real desire, which is to be one with the Divine. This desire is like a glowing golden seed that is nestled deep in your heart, and once it is found, it can blossom into beauty, strength, and lasting fulfillment in your life.

Living behind a facade is unsustainable, because nothing of value can emerge when you are only focused on either making your self-image more beautiful or successful or making it more inconspicuous, so it is small and unthreatening to others. No matter how good you are at doing either of those, the one thing you can't control is another person's reaction to that facade. Two hundred people can like and praise the created self, but then the two who don't will exacerbate the very feelings of sadness and rejection it was created to cover over.

On top of that, the facade is never real and true. You create that role out of your primal longing for oneness and love, but the experience you are seeking cannot come from acceptance by others. It can only come through the recognition of the Divine within you. True worth and acceptance can only be sourced from your soul.

> *True worth and acceptance can only be sourced from your soul.*

The individual's search for worth, acceptance, and love is humanity's search for belonging. It is one massive, primordial cry for love that resounds over all continents, across all oceans. The emptiness you feel is the catalyst, the wake-up call, the trigger that allows the

need for belonging to become the yearning for connection, authenticity, and oneness. That process begins
when you start to become more conscious of the illusion that is the created self and recognize that truth
lives in the Essential Self.

2

The Possibility

N 1957, A MONASTERY IN THAILAND WAS BEING RE-
located. A group of monks was charged with moving a
giant clay Buddha. This assignment required meticulous care and attention. As they were preparing to move
it, one of them noticed a crack in the clay. Concerned
about damaging it further, they decided to wait a day
before continuing. Later, a single monk came to do a
closer inspection with the help of a flashlight. To his

amazement, he noticed a sliver of pure gold glinting in the crack. Taking a hammer and chisel, he carefully began tapping, not sure what he would find. After hours and hours of work, as the old clay crumbled away, the true beauty and original integrity of the Buddha was revealed. Standing before the monk was a solid gold statue.

Historians believe that, centuries earlier, the Buddha had been covered in layers of clay to protect it from an impending attack by the Burmese army. It wasn't until hundreds of years later that this great treasure was rediscovered in all its original magnificence. Its true glory had been there all along, finally revealed by a crack in its protective layer. The whole process of revelation was facilitated by grace.

Grace powers revelation. Grace is the sacred energy that creates expansion and the possibility of recognition of your Essential Self. There is grace in every situation. It shows up in countless forms. Whether you are standing in line at a movie theater, dealing with your crying baby, mourning the death of a loved one, or in the midst of the inevitable highs and lows of marriage or divorce, the power to reveal the Essential Self is always present.

Grace especially loves synchronicity. The monks in the monastery experienced grace in that crack in the clay.

Indeed, for Divine Consciousness, the overarching energy within which all life is unfolding, to impact you, there has to be a crack in the fear-based shell, so that the Divine Essence that dwells at your core can emerge. Think of Divine Consciousness as the ocean, and your Divine Essence as a drop of water. What's inside is what's outside, and what's outside is what's inside. This crack is the start of an awakening. It is the necessary catalyst that allows the drop of water to once again merge with the ocean. It is the opening that allows grace to permeate your life—gently, sublimely, profoundly. Yet people often overlook the importance of the accident.

Often, the precursor to spiritual awakening is some crisis, something that cuts through the thick layers of illusion of the ego. Someone leaves you. You contract a serious illness. You have a falling-out with your closest friend. You deal with an addiction. You lose money. And then, out of the perceived constrictions, out of the darkness you are experiencing in the external, the internal eye rouses from its slumber. It awakens to facilitate the emergence of the transcendent beauty and joy that you could not see in the chaos and perceived limitation. There is an intervention, a release, a glimmer of truth, a shift in perception. You begin to see life with new eyes and an open heart.

Often, the precursor to spiritual awakening is some crisis, something that cuts through the thick layers of illusion of the ego.

Sometimes you experience the crack in your egoic structure that allows the light of your Divine Essence to emerge, but you write it off. You don't want to look into the crack because doing so is uncomfortable. You turn your attention to something else—your news feed, a drama in your life or someone else's, the TV, or online shopping. You find some distraction, any distraction.

But there comes a time when you are curious enough to ask, "What is that?" There is a part of you that wants to look into the crack—that is the mystic in you. That is you being courageous enough to explore what seems to be the unknowable: the Essential Self. Spirituality is opening the door to grace.

The depth of your being is so vast. It is unfathomably powerful, and you are constantly revealing it. The Essential Self is consciousness, the Observer, the Witness. It is the universal, soulful aspect of you that stretches into infinity in all directions, beyond time and space.

Your Buddha nature, your luminosity, has been hidden

from your awareness by the conditioning and wounding that you have experienced throughout your life. The result is the separation from your Essential Self. I am taking you on a journey of awakening that will allow you to become conscious of how you moved into that separation, how you have gone from wholeness to woundedness. Then I will show you the possibility of a return to the remembrance, realization, and illumination of your essence.

The depth of your being is so vast.
It is unfathomably powerful, and you are
constantly revealing it.

Knowing your Essential Self is not about how you look or your IQ. It's not about your killer personality, how many exotic stamps mark up your passport, what degrees you've earned, or the money you've made. It's not about the philanthropic work you've accomplished or the hours you meditate or pray. It's not even about the children you've brought into this world. The Essential Self cannot be damaged, won, or lost. It is the eternal prism through which the Divine uniquely expresses itself in this world. It is the foundation of peace and fulfillment.

Perhaps a little peace and fulfillment sound relieving, like taking a deep breath of fresh air after being cooped up all day or a sip of cool water on a sweltering midsummer's afternoon. But what I am talking about is much more than a minor reprieve. Within your Essential Self lies a possibility that is all-inclusive. You can have everything.

By "everything" I mean so much more than material comforts or achievements. I mean the restoration of wholeness, the return to the peace of being you as you were intended to be—in union with Divine Consciousness. This restoration redefines what it means to be human. The light of consciousness eliminates the illusory stories, false identities, unconscious patterns, and unresolved memories that reside in the very cells of your body. It also dissolves the sadness, fears, and anger that bubble up from your depths.

Currently, the false narrative about what it means to be human is defined by suffering, limitation, and fear. It includes feelings of separateness and an unending struggle to fulfill yourself through relationships, physical possessions, and achievement. It also includes feelings of victimhood, the pervasive feeling that life is happening to you and that you are powerless to make any real changes—all of which leads to dissatisfaction.

Sometimes, the dissatisfaction is very subtle, like a faint odor that has become normalized in your experience. You didn't order the right dish at the restaurant, so you spend the entire meal completely distracted, watching what other people ordered and wondering what they all taste like, rather than being fully present with your spouse.

Your best friend raves about her meditation class, so you quit yours to join hers, but now you find that you are not experiencing the same degree of results. You spend the whole class, which is supposed to be dedicated to expanding your consciousness, feeling agitated and wondering if you've made a mistake.

You are second-guessing the outfit you bought for your best friend's birthday party. Is it the right color? Too fancy? Too tight? If you had shopped longer, could you have found one that was less expensive? You're always shopping, returning, and repurchasing in order to find what will make you look to others how you want to feel inside. You justify it all by saying you have high standards, but the truth is you are attempting to manufacture comfort, assurance, satisfaction, and self-worth externally.

This theme also undermines your relationships, preventing the partner in front of you from receiving a fair chance. Your friend receives an engagement ring on the second anniversary of meeting her partner. Your partner refuses to make a commitment even though you've been dating the same amount of time. Your mind never stops creating and reordering the list of qualities this person should be exhibiting, while reinforcing your belief that you are a total failure at choosing partners. You are becoming convinced there must be someone better out there for you.

Your marriage is far from solid, and now your wife has reconnected with an old college boyfriend via social media. She seems happier to have found him after all these years than she is every evening when you walk through the door after a long hard day of work. You've been cheated on before and jump to the conclusion that this scenario will ultimately send you down the same path. You begin to consider divorce, so that you aren't the one who gets left in the dirt this time.

The restoration of authenticity puts an end to all these mind games. In this restoration, your peace is independent of outside factors. When you are embodying your Essential Self, *any choice you make is the right one*, in all scenarios. There is no room for complaints or uncertainty. An energy of deep continuity and profound connection pervades your everyday existence. You stand on a stronger, higher inner platform, in awe of life in its many forms. Dissatisfaction falls away like dead foliage taken up in a gust of spring wind.

> *When you are embodying your Essential Self, any choice you make is the right one, in all scenarios. There is no room for complaints or uncertainty.*

The restoration also includes the reestablishment of the joy of living and gratitude for what was once taken for granted: eyes to see the faces of those you love, ears to hear the laughter of your child, legs to go for a morning jog, and lungs to breathe deeply and fully. There is an awareness of the limitless possibilities constantly emerging in the spaciousness of the present moment: short exchanges with people you hardly know, hearing your favorite song after a long day's work, time to write in your journal, a feeling of closeness to nature and the higher force therein.

To be authentically human is to hold within your conscious experience the attributes of joy, abundance, peace, love, and fulfillment—to be connected to the universe—to live in the flow and momentum of the world around you. All of this is your birthright. This is the real possibility.

When there is a room filled with darkness and you are uncomfortable in its folds, the first response is to resist or try to control it. When that doesn't work, the next response is to push it away, which is physically impossible. Then you try to negotiate, which proves utterly useless. When that also fails, it becomes an all-out war. But the darkness doesn't respond. The darkness remains. In the same way, your propensity is to fight, resist, or control the things that don't look like what you have been conditioned to believe are the paths to happiness. You fight the inadequacy, limitations, suffering, and everything you fear. But your fight never brings peace.

We all want to be loved, accepted, and worthy. And so you have accepted conditioning and obscured your Essential Self, favoring a disguise. You live in separation, seeing the world as me and you, us and them, friend and enemy, right and wrong. You spend a lot of time trying to appear certain ways to certain people, as if you need to manipulate the world into recognizing your value. You are "nice," because that is what you were taught to be. There is a polite veneer. You grasp at the false promise. You live in the past and future. You distract yourself from the pain with alcohol, drugs, gambling, sex, social media, and more. Sadness begins to grow. You get therapy, read self-help books, and attend countless seminars or retreats. You get temporary bouts of relief, but eventually darkness surrounds you again. It seems almost cruelly impassive about your efforts.

How do you eliminate the darkness? With a second principle. You turn on the light—or in your case, you uncover the true light of the Essential Self. What this means is that you turn your attention from the dissonance and cacophony of the exterior world and become conscious of everything within—the discomfort and discord, the internal states that make you want to run or hide.

You shine the light of awareness upon your feelings, thoughts, and motivations, just as that monk shined his flashlight on the crack in the statue. You begin to see what you have been running from, pushing away, and resisting. You stop trying to leach satisfaction from anything and everything outside of yourself. You start to inquire into the nature of your script rather than just blindly acting it out. As your conscious awareness increases, the clay crumbles and your natural luminosity reveals itself, real gold in broad daylight.

The darkness you deal with is separation. Your separation is forgetting your Essential Self, veiling the authentic you, living in a created self. Underneath that role you play, underneath the darkness you see, underneath the sadness you feel is your luminous Buddha nature. The real promise, the true possibility, is living in that light, samadhi. When the light is turned on, the darkness evaporates. It's not fighting and winning a battle. It's not altering the darkness or fixing something that is broken. You are enough as you are.

Reveal the light, banish the darkness.

3

Conditioning

NONE OF US WILLINGLY CHOOSE DARKNESS. THIS
situation where you moved from authenticity to
inauthenticity came to be because of what you
have experienced. It came about because of conditioning
and wounding.

Do you remember a time when you were very young,
a time of innocence? A time when life was so simple,
playful, and free? There was no pressure to be anything

other than you. You didn't think about what other people thought of you. You didn't see differences between you and your friends. There was just simple, unbounded, authentic, and natural joy.

In this stage of life, you play in the park for hours with no concept of time. You build sandcastles at the seashore, only to watch them wash away in the waves. You sit in the grass, wiggle your toes in the mud, and giggle and laugh out loud. You feel free. Very often you get lost in your own world of make-believe—an innocent child becoming a ballerina, a superhero, or a cowboy. Life is simple, flowing with love, peace, curiosity, discovery, and fulfillment.

But then you break the window in the living room by mistake. Your father screams. For the first time ever, you are told you are bad. You experience fear. You feel shame. Your foundation of safety is shattered. More than anything, you desperately want his love and approval.

You are not invited to a birthday party. Your classmates are talking about it with anticipation and excitement. You feel excluded, alone, confused, and different, like the "ugly duckling" in the book your mom used to read to you. When Monday morning comes, you overhear the children recounting the fun activities you missed out on. An unknown emotion burns just below your rib cage and rises up as a lump in your throat. It tastes bitter, like the tears you will not allow yourself to cry. You learn to swallow hard. You want desperately to fit in. You want to be accepted and avoid rejection.

Your parents fight a lot. They are not happy. You can feel your mother's sadness as if it is your own. Hurtful words fly through the air like arrows to the heart. Maybe there is a divorce. Whatever it is, it is somehow your fault. You feel you must have misbehaved or else you are just a bad child. Fear and guilt wind themselves through your little body like a venomous snake. You desperately want to be loved and feel safe again.

You vow to be a good girl or boy. And not just good—you will be perfect. You will do everything you can to keep your parents happy and your teachers pleased, to keep that insidious snake at bay. You become very sensitive to other people's emotional states, developing a keen awareness of what to say and what not to say, when to leave and when to stay in order to manage the energy around you as best you can. You do anything to avoid making waves.

Everything amounts to a good show. When you feel sad, you run to the bathroom and cry. Once in a while, something will trigger anger. But when you lash out at your siblings, you soon realize that you just end up punished and alone. You learn to hide your true feelings or only show them reluctantly on occasion. A fake smile becomes one of your best weapons of defense. You are very careful of what you allow others to see. When you feel bad, you stuff it down as tightly as possible.

And it isn't just your feelings. Fueled by your unresolved emotional energy, your peaceful mind becomes agitated. It becomes compulsive, creating unending scenarios that you could fear and worry about. The incessant mental chatter becomes the dictator in your head, an unrelenting inner voice that can't be quieted: "Why did you say that? Now they will never like you. What are you thinking? They were right, you are stupid! What a loser." It never rests. You worry what others will say or do. To escape, you move into living in the past and future instead of the present moment.

You are told you are a sinner, and you must be saved. If you don't get saved, if you don't watch out, you might be sent to hell for all eternity. But what about the time you spilled your orange juice all over the breakfast table, it ran down your leg and onto the floor, and your mother became so angry? Or all the times you didn't feel like feeding the family cat you had promised to take care of? Or all the times you didn't do your homework and lied about forgetting it at home. These experiences flash across your mind as you consider sin. You decide you are unworthy.

It's the middle-school formal, and everyone has been asked to dance but you. You are not handsome enough, not pretty enough, not thin enough. You are not in the right social circle. You decide you will do whatever it takes to create a new version of yourself for the next year. Summer break becomes an all-out effort to become skinny, more charming, and funnier. No matter what, you must gain approval and acceptance.

Eventually you learn the power of sarcasm, even at the expense of other people's feelings. You use your sensitivity to your advantage, knowing just what to say and what not to say to make sure you are liked and get what you need. It is manipulation for the sake of surviving, for the sake of protecting this fragile little being who was never good enough.

You create a strong exterior, a covering, a shell— one that is worthy of social acceptance and the world's praise. It is a shining suit of armor you don each morning, but it has started to mold to your skin. Underneath you hate that little girl or boy who didn't have what it took, who was clumsy, weak, or incompetent.

Consciously or unconsciously, you judge this child as the source of your misery. If this child had been better, tougher, smarter, and more acceptable, you wouldn't have suffered. So you begin to live in a created self, a facade that you think will be loved.

As a young teen, you begin to explore your identity,

your sexuality, and how you fit in socially. You hide your pimples with makeup and start to swear. More than anything, you just want to look and be cool. But when you touch your own body and it feels good, there is guilt. In church, they say sex is bad. Since you are experiencing these new sensations, you unconsciously surmise you must be bad also. Shame sets in.

In high school, you become an overachiever, an underachiever, a rebel, a perfectionist. You also take on a role—pretty girl, nerd, jock, thespian, cool kid, clown, the mean girl, the emo, or the "friends with everybody" floater. No matter what, you've already felt the chains of your own conditioning and begin to rebel. But even in your new role, in this "liberated" persona, you still feel confined, because you are in reaction and resistance to yourself and your reality.

From the moment you were born, throughout your childhood, early adolescence, and late teens, you have been conditioned out of your authenticity and away from your Divine Essence. You have been influenced and altered, so you could please others. You have conformed, learning to live from fear, inadequacy, and scarcity, because those are the energies that dominate the world you live in, where it is wrong to get angry, to feel sadness, to feel pain. You created a facade that was good enough.

From the moment you were born,
throughout your childhood, early adolescence,
and late teens, you have been conditioned
out of your authenticity and away
from your Divine Essence.

Everywhere you looked, there it was—conditioning, an insidious control mechanism that makes you believe you must think, look, speak, and act a certain way to gain love and acceptance. You sought it from your parents, but that was conditional upon your behavior. You sought it from friends, but that was conditional upon how well you were able to navigate tricky social dynamics.

You sought it from religion, but that was conditional upon how closely you followed the rules and commandments. You sought it from work, but that was conditional upon your performance. You sought it from society, but that was conditional upon your degrees, salary bracket, and accomplishments.

And then you tried to find love and acceptance in your relationship, perhaps the most painful place of all. You needed someone else to see you, to recognize the beauty and depth that you had denied. But even when you found a boyfriend or girlfriend, you were not able to receive their love, because you believed you were unworthy. There was shame in your imperfection.

You became a master of camouflage, a chameleon. You became so good at adapting to what people expected from you that you started to forget your real colors. You never really let another person see who you were—your flaws, the "awful" things you had done, the mistakes you made. If others saw the real you, there is no way they could still feel love for you. Over and over, you found people who would dance your dance, but the final movements were always the same—some form of betrayal, abandonment, or rejection.

The software of this social programming, of conditioning, is language. It's everything you were told, taught, pressured to believe, and instructed was right and acceptable. That engineering was married with heightened emotion. It was how you were controlled through the power of acceptance or rejection. You were the soft, gentle child who was molded to conform to a way of thinking, acting, and believing. You were pressured into creating that facade.

Let's look at an example of how insidious these control mechanisms are. Society uses heightened language when talking about sex, which then creates a heightened emotional response—shame or guilt—which is then intended to create some form of sexual conformity within the child. This is what is acceptable. If you fall outside these parameters, then we are going to give you the human equivalent of what we give to lab rats. Instead of giving you an electric shock, we'll bestow a visceral emotional response amplified through the language we have conditioned you with that makes you feel bad. If you follow what we are saying precisely, we will give you the blessing, the reward, the acceptance, the love.

That's conditioning, social engineering, programming. And it is not just with sex; it's with everything. It is the conditioning that creates a facade you live behind, masking your Essential Self.

It is the conditioning that creates a facade you live behind, masking your Essential Self.

There are very few people who can totally conform to this conditioning. The box is too narrow, too confining. In order to be totally acceptable, you have to suppress what is authentically you. You have to constantly reject yourself in order to belong in society. You are told what is right and wrong. Through a variety of mediums including TV, movies, magazines, and the internet, you are told what success means, what it means to be attractive, what it means to be successful, and what love is supposed to look like.

Buried deep underneath that facade and that pain is your Divine Essence. You have covered it up and forgotten your Essential Self in a vain outward search for something that no one and nothing in this world could give you. After all, how can you hold a planet full of people who don't love or accept themselves responsible for loving and accepting you?

> *How can you hold a planet full of people*
> *who don't love or accept themselves*
> *responsible for loving and accepting you?*

The time has come for you to stop seeking acceptance in places you will never find it and finally surrender to the peace that you are. Liberation from this created, conditioned self is the path to transcendent peace, love, health, abundance, and joy. It is the ultimate threshold to freedom.

4

Your Core Wounding

THE DETAILS ARE INCONSEQUENTIAL. IN FACT, YOU may not even remember what happened. What is important is that there was some pivotal juncture in your formative years when you first realized that your Essential Self did not fit into the conditioning of the world into which you were born. It was a moment of emotional torment and upheaval, imprinted on your being like a vibrational energetic tattoo. You were not safe.

You were somehow unlovable. You did not measure up. You were experiencing fear. You were all alone.

Simultaneously with that event, a deep sense of unworthiness entered your vibrational sphere and became cemented in place by shame and guilt. Several more similar experiences piled on that initial one, and the accumulation resulted in a more generalized feeling that, no matter what, you weren't worthy of the goodness that life has to offer. This unworthiness is your core wounding, and it has shaped your entire life from its inception.

Most of the decisions you make, the goals you pursue, the relationships you desire, and the life you are creating are motivated by a need to compensate for your core wounding through a search for love, approval, acceptance, and adulation from the outside world. Through the years, you may have developed a sweet demeanor to make sure you are pleasing to others or perhaps you have perfected the art of flattery. You may enshroud yourself in an air of false humility (which is really just making yourself small to keep other people happy and comfortable).

Perhaps you decide to become a perfect disciple in the hopes that holiness will be your savior. Or a social reformer out to change the world. Or maybe you strive to be the shining example of excellent parenthood. But since all of this striving is outwardly focused, dependent upon others or rooted in shame, you never find what you are looking for.

Over and over, you wind up rejected, betrayed, abandoned, or simply disappointed. Even when you find success making a lot of money, becoming famous, or finding the perfect mate, you are not truly fulfilled by it. There is a lingering desperation, a sadness that is attached to you like your shadow. It is not enough. You are not enough.

At thirty-five years old, you meet with your boss for your yearly performance review. You have kissed up to those in power, overachieved at the cost of relationships with family and friends, worked late nights and weekends, and scraped and clawed for a promotion. You are a perfectionist, because it is only in perfection that you are worthy of approval. You have done everything you possibly could have to make yourself invaluable to your boss. But then he tells you someone else got the promotion. Your mind goes into victimhood, judgment, anger, revenge. And beneath all of that is a sense of weighty despair.

At forty years old, you have strived to be the perfect parent. You sacrificed for your children and spent countless sleepless nights caring for them. You jeopardized your retirement for their education and then went to counseling to make it all better. You expected they would return your effort, but now your son never calls, and your daughter just told you she's dropping out of school and doesn't want to hear your opinion.

At the foundation of it all, there is a rising fear. It can be so subtle that you don't even realize how much it is fueling your existence. It is a fear that you will lose your power, money, and position. Fear that you will be lonely, unloved, and forgotten. Fear that you will be uncovered as a sham. Fear of disease. Fear of loss. Fear that your flaws will be exposed for all to judge. These fears keep you up at night.

At fifty, you are shocked when your spouse files for divorce. You did everything for your partner. You did your share of household duties and worked full-time. You dressed for your spouse, spoke the way that was pleasing, supported his or her goals, and made sacrifices, too many to count. Now your spouse wants to leave you. In your mind you think, "I failed. I look too old. I am not smart enough. I complained too much. I am no longer desirable. I am un-lovable." This single act confirms your unworthiness, and your world collapses. Depression arises from the rubble.

Over the years, you successfully avoided these feel-ings. You tried to quiet the thoughts in your head—with alcohol, drugs, or exercise. Maybe it was gambling, sex, overworking, overeating, getting lost in TV and movies, pornography, or social media. You became a master of distraction and escape. There were the antidepressants, which blunted the feelings. Or perhaps you developed an addiction, turning your rage on yourself, as you attempted to control a situation that was uncontrollable and unwinnable.

Because you would never show anyone who you really were, intimacy was impossible. You could have been surrounded by a group of the most loving people in the world, a spiritual community perhaps or your family, but you still felt alone. Perhaps you lived in one of the largest cities, amid the busy bustle of millions of other souls, but since you eluded yourself, deep connections with others eluded you also.

> *Because you would never show anyone who you really were, intimacy was impossible.*

It was the same in your personal relationships. No matter how enticing the initial chemistry, you were never able to experience the depth of connection you craved.

You kept trying to fix the other person because it made your existence feel worthwhile, but eventually he or she crushed you by resisting your "help." You also feared showing the "unacceptable" parts of yourself. You feared being seen as needy. But mostly you feared the sting of rejection.

Your core wounding is separation from self-love, which results in deep feelings of unworthiness. The healing of that wounding is a journey back to your Essential Self. In order to begin the journey, you have to turn and face this unworthiness. The thorn can only be removed by finding and facing it, acknowledging its power over you, however brief. What you have been doing is looking away from your core wounding, distracting yourself by making more money, changing relationships, focusing on "self-improvement," instead of creating an inner focus on the one thing that really needs your attention and can make the difference.

> *Your core wounding is separation from self-love, which results in deep feelings of unworthiness. The healing of that wounding is a journey back to your Essential Self.*

The energy of fear and the struggle to survive generate an internal feeling most people spend their whole lives avoiding. Freedom comes from giving that feeling your conscious attention, without judgment. Your willingness to surrender to the feeling of unworthiness, unlovability, or not being enough is the crack that allows grace to enter.

In conscious attention lies your power to create real transformation. The Indian philosopher J. Krishnamurti wrote, "The highest form of intelligence is the ability to observe yourself without evaluating." It is in this judgment-free state of observation that the concentrated power of your pure potential resides.

Over the decades, you lost connection to your Essential Self. You may be internally bruised from years of self-loathing, resentment, regret, and the aggravation of never being able to fully feel that who you are and what you have to offer is enough. The blessing of this pain is that it has drawn you to the search for truth. It is the inner, sometimes unconscious yearning for a remembrance of and return to your Essential Self that draws grace and illumination into your life and ignites the possibility of enlightenment and the return to authenticity.

It is the inner, sometimes unconscious yearning for a remembrance of and return to your Essential Self that draws grace and illumination into your life and ignites the possibility of enlightenment and the return to authenticity.

Some people think enlightenment is a pie-in-the-sky place where you go when you've meditated long enough or done enough good deeds. But in truth, enlightenment is a vibrational realignment of energy that unfolds as you shed your inauthenticity and return to who you are.

It is not always neat and pretty, but it is a raw and real process that restores integrity and worthiness from within. It eradicates suffering. It is the embodiment of true love, joy, and connection. It is your samadhi.

Ultimately it is the gift of real freedom.

5

The Essential Self

YOUR ESSENTIAL SELF IS VAST. IT IS PURE CON-
sciousness, universal awareness, and it is the
foundation of all expression, creativity, and expansion in this world. It is "you" in your most unadul-
terated form. You entered this world with this essential
innocence and purity, but life's events have distanced and
covered over the core foundation of your being. You have
forgotten the *essential you.*

When you forget, you do something very curious. You experience your mind thinking, your feelings arising, and your body functioning, and you conclude that those aspects of your experience are the totality of who you are. You say, "I'm fat," "I'm depressed," "I'm poor, broken, and hopeless," "I'm angry," or "I'm stupid," as if you *are* the thought, feeling, situation, or body part. But these are misidentifications, ones that cause unnecessary pain and perpetuate limitations. You have been conditioned to overly identify with your mind and body, and this conditioning has imprisoned your being.

Descartes's famous maxim *Cogito ergo sum* ("I think; therefore I am") has become the basis of modern Western philosophy. Instead of a holistic identification with multidimensional aspects of the Essential Self, the thinking mind is our primary indicator of existence. Over the course of the previous century, brain function itself became one of the primary foci of scientific inquiry. And today, too often society treats disturbances such as anxiety and depression as issues solely of brain chemistry. On top of that, Western psychology grew increasingly preoccupied with "the power of positive thinking," which became the basis of the highly influential spiritual movement called New Thought.

But being solely oriented toward the mind is limiting. It does not take into account the complete vibrational makeup of the individual. Yes, the mind is a part of who you are, but there is also the core foundation of Being—*an awareness that can observe, interact, and formulate thought patterns.* In his definitive assessment, Descartes missed the fundamental truth: "I am; therefore I think." The "I am" is Being or Soul, which represents the totality of our potential.

When you think, "I am rich," what you have is a thought with limited power, because it has a limited connection to its source, the soul. You can think or say a million times, "I am rich," but very rarely will this type of mental exercise create palpable change. It's like bemoaning living in the dark, all the while residing next to a power station, or having access to electricity, but never turning on the lights. Just as the power station represents potential connection, Being, once accessed, powers the transformative process. Until your mental desires are aligned with the power of Being, they cannot come into existence.

Our current culture idolizes the body as the home of worthiness and the seat of the self; witness exercise as religion, extreme diets, medical procedures for cosmetic reasons, selfies, and a preoccupation with celebrities. Statistics show that large numbers of individuals are unhappy with their physical size and shape, even if it is healthy and strong. And although the psychological impact of social media has not yet been totally realized, there is no doubt that it fuels a cultural obsession with appearance and superficiality.

Even spirituality these days is shallow, focused on the body and mind. Eastern mysticism has been made more palatable to the Western outlook, and much of the depth and purpose has been lost in translation. Hatha Yoga, one of the oldest and most profound of practices, has become about the body, stretching, and aerobics—a gym workout. Many workshops and "spiritual retreats" focus on getting people to obtain certain results—more money, a relationship, a slimmer figure—but few of them focus on connecting individuals to their soul, that eternal part of Being beyond the confines of time and space.

The ego appropriates "spiritual" activities, but waters them down, rendering them ineffective, ensuring that nothing changes too much. Anything that threatens the status quo or has the power to transform is demonized, because it threatens the larger egoic structure. People will read a book about transformation or learn a technique, but few will go beyond that and launch an all-out mission to find and reveal their soul.

But all of that is about to change. The ways in which humans have identified the seat of the self have moved in phases. These phases are evolutionary. Now the time has come for the phase of soul identification. You have a mind and you have a body, but in truth you are Soul.

You are Being experiencing the mind and body. This remembrance of Soul is a maturation into the truth of the Eastern mystics. The complete transformational paradigm now coming up on the horizon requires the inclusion of the Essential Self as a foundational element. It is a wave of conscious human evolution—an expansion of awareness into the depth of wholeness. Until the soul is fully liberated and revealed, it cannot display its full power and potential in your life. The soul is the only part of you that has enough power to transform you. Identification as Soul and embodying the state of samadhi are the next evolutionary frontiers.

When you accept living in a world where you experience only a very limited part of who you truly are, it's disconcerting. You can't figure it out, but you know something's missing. You know, deep inside, there is more. Your mind tries ceaselessly to find peace and fulfillment externally, because that's where you've been told to look. A frantic search ensues. Your mind drives you crazy trying to figure it out—planning, imagining, worrying, being angry, feeling lost. Meanwhile, you believe all those thoughts are "you."

> *When you accept living in a world where you experience only a very limited part of who you truly are, it's disconcerting. You can't figure it out, but you know something's missing. You know, deep inside, there is more.*

But you *can* take a step back and watch your thoughts float by, in the same way that you can observe an aquarium teeming with brightly colored tropical fish and crawling creatures. Are you the fish with their resplendent flowing fins? Of course not. You are the one watching them dart and cleave through the water. You are not the thoughts themselves; you are the Observer. The Observer, that awareness, is your Essential Self.

One moment you love a person and the next you hate that person. But when the love seems to disappear, do you disappear also? No. You are still here, nursing your breakup in bed with a carton of Ben and Jerry's or a package of Oreos. No matter how much pain you are in or how many hot tears stream down your face in the moments of your deepest despair, you are not your sadness or your heartache. Nor are you the infatuation you feel, or the fear, the hatred, the laughter.

As the Observer, you can sense your feelings emerging and subsiding, just as you can sit at the water's edge and feel the cold waves washing over your toes one moment and then receding the next. Emotions are a part of your experience and you allow yourself to feel them through to completion, but they do not control you; nor are you defined by them. And then they pass.

Every morning you put your two feet on the floor next to your bed. Most likely the first thing you do is head toward the bathroom. In the mirror, you take a look at yourself—a quick glance at your face. Who is looking back at you? As you get into the shower, you assess your hips, your thighs, your backside. You identify as that body, and you think that body is too pudgy, too out of shape, or too wrinkled. The assessment awakens an internal emotional reaction, and in that experience you unconsciously come to the conclusion: "This is who I am." But the body is not the Essential Self. And yet you constantly reinforce the idea that it is.

Think about how it feels to identify as a body that is never perfect, always aging, often suffering, and eventually dying. Think about what it's like to identify as chaotic thoughts—some happy, some irrational, some hateful, some incoherent, and some cogent. Think about how it feels to identify as emotions that sometimes overpower you and at other times make you run away. It's a roller-coaster existence that could make anyone crazy. When the body is in its prime, when the mind is calm for thirty seconds, and when you feel happy, all is well. But the other 99.8 percent of the time, it's a bit insane.

No wonder you feel unworthy and sad. You have obscured your Essential Self and identified with a created self and the body, mind, and emotions—all of which are in constant flux. This limited identification lacks a strong foundation. Imagine for a minute one of the most awe-inspiring, innovative skyscrapers in the world, glittering against the night sky, dominating an urban landscape. Now imagine that this award-winning, provocatively modern tower was built on sand, without reinforced concrete and steel footings. When a building lacks a solid foundation, collapse is imminent.

The same thing happens in your life. In this state of separation from your Essential Self, you may feel internally weak, as if you might fall to pieces at the onset of any sort of difficulty or criticism. Any pushback that life delivers takes you out. You experience feelings of worthlessness and live in resistance to and judgment of your thoughts, feelings, appearance, and surroundings. And then you stay there, because you have been conditioned to hold on to whatever is "normal" with every fiber of your being, even when normal is chaos, dysfunctional relationships, or lack of financial security. You cling to the familiar, even if it is just mediocre. You cling because the created self's greatest fear is the unknown.

> *You have been conditioned to hold on to whatever is "normal" with every fiber of your being, even when normal is chaos, dysfunctional relationships, or lack of financial security. You cling to the familiar, even if it is just mediocre. You cling because the created self's greatest fear is the unknown.*

Life can never fool you again. Although it will try relentlessly to convince you that there are endless obstacles to achieving your greatest desires, you are now awakened.

You can't be dissuaded. The distractions that once kept you in the dark are slowly losing their power over you.

When you willingly reconnect to your Essential Self—to your soul—you immediately access the power and potential for unimaginable transformation. This power requires no effort, no pushing, no striving. It is the most natural experience of all, and yet because we have been conditioned to move so far away from it, the experience feels completely foreign.

> *When you willingly reconnect to your Essential Self—to your soul—you immediately access the power and potential for unimaginable transformation. This power requires no effort, no pushing, no striving.*

Your beautiful mind, your perfect body, your expressive emotions—they are what make you unique. They are all the vehicles of your soul.

6

Vibrational Transformation

HAVE YOU EVER TRIED A "POSITIVE THINKING" method to make something happen in your life, only to find it ended up getting you nowhere? Let's say you have a deep desire to create financial wealth and independence. You visualize yourself sitting on piles and piles of cash. You repeat, "I am rich," over and over and over again. You paste yellow sticky notes with this mantra on your bathroom mirror.

You make a vision board featuring everything your financial independence will provide: the car, the house, bills marked "paid," and a photo of a happy you without financial worry. You picture yourself earning a large bonus. You even make out a check to yourself for a million dollars, frame it, and hang it above your desk. But when the end of the month comes around, you are still behind on your payments.

Now, what about waking up out of a dead sleep at three in the morning overcome with anxiety, drenched in sweat, and short of breath? How often have you tried to slow down an avalanche of worrisome thoughts through sheer willpower? Your nerves are frayed, and you feel sick to your stomach. One bleak scenario after another plays out in your mind. Your adrenaline is pumping. But the more you tell yourself not to worry, not to worry, not to worry, the more anxious you become.

If you've attempted to effect change by trying to control your mind, only to wind up tired and frustrated, you are not alone. Creating change solely through mental techniques is impossible. It is like treating only the surface of an open wound when the infection is deep inside.

It's only when you address the underlying energy holding these thoughts and beliefs in place that you can effectively create transformation. That is why I say a shift in energy is always followed by a change in reality. Your life is an exact reflection of your overall vibrational frequency. To experience authentic transformation is to find a new way of being and relating in the world, one that is anchored in your soul.

The late and blessed Wayne Dyer once said, "When you squeeze an orange, you'll always get orange juice to come out. What comes out is what's inside." This means that if you have denser energies like bitterness, anger, or frustration lying dormant in your vibrational system, then situations will occur in your outer reality—perhaps a criticism, betrayal, or delay—in order to allow those energies to be brought to the surface, felt, and released.

Someone can only make you angry or sad if you already have the vibrations of anger and sadness within you. When you oppose someone, *it is an energy within yourself that you are opposing*. When your "buttons get pushed," *it is because the buttons are there in the first place*.

You experience repetitive negative patterns in your life, because you have not dealt with the unresolved parts of yourself. You face yet another dead-end job, another tyrannical employer. You divorce and remarry another, only to find yourself in the exact same position. You bring in money, only to have it seemingly slip through your fingers—again.

Vibrational transformation is a powerful internal process that addresses embedded, unresolved vibrations—dense emotional content and conditioning—and changes them from a dissonant vibration into a harmonious vibration through the conscious acceptance of the root cause of the unconscious dissonance. Then your reality begins to reflect that change, and real and lasting personal transformation can occur. Dissolve your sadness, your anger, your pain, your unworthiness, and you will no longer need external circumstances to stir them from the depths and show you that they are there.

Most people try to remedy the shortfalls in their life externally—"I don't have a relationship, so I'll take a workshop on how to get one"—which is only another distraction. Even if they find a new relationship, they struggle to keep it for the long term. When people attempt to transform as a way to manage external reality—to change or fix themselves and their circumstances—they miss a critical truth. *You don't need to be fixed. You are perfect as you are.* You need only to restore connection to your Essential Self to remember your divine blueprint.

> *You don't need to be fixed.*
> *You are perfect as you are.*

Transformation must be addressed from an energy standpoint. Vibrational transformation turns your focus inward, supports you in the integration of your core wounding, and facilitates the dynamic emergence of your soul. When transformation is vibrational, the symptoms of separation resolve themselves, because you have addressed the source.

What is the source of all human suffering? A lack of connection to the Essential Self, a lack of connection to the Divine. As St. Francis of Assisi so beautifully phrased it, "We are all in mourning for the experience of our essence we knew and now miss. Light is the cure; all else a placebo." Vibrational transformation provides connection to that light that frees you from suffering and produces an expansion and an increase in every area of your life.

One of the symptoms of forgetting the Essential Self is the monkey mind, a mind constantly in motion, distracted from the present moment by incessant chattering thoughts that drag you into the past or thrust you into the future. Another is your sense of unworthiness. Another is false identification as your thoughts, emotions, and body. Another is feeling separate. Another is limitation. The cause of this is the unresolved, dense vibrational energy that is locked within you. This separates you from the light, and this is the reason you have forgotten the biggest and most essential part of yourself.

Let's take a look at an example. Your partner just told you that he or she is going to leave you. Within you there exists the possibility for either a conditioned reaction or a conscious response. The conditioned reaction is a formulation of all the constructs you have gathered from society, religion, your upbringing, and your experiences. The conditioned reaction is based in the egoic belief that the other person is a possession, an extension of your fabricated self. It is codependency. It is what creates the pain of being left. Without codependency, the reality of the situation is that your partner is simply leaving. But instead of seeing it as an evolution of the relationship, you personalize it according to the conditioning that language has imposed on your created self: "Why is this happening to me? Look at what you did to me."

Statements of victimhood become your story, who you are. You are then locked into the conditioned reaction, and the result is that there is no freedom to deal with the circumstance. You have personalized it. And in that personalization, there is tremendous, almost irreconcilable pain.

You have a subtle nervous system that acts like an airplane's black box, where every experience of your life is vibrationally recorded. Every experience creates an energy impression in your nervous system. These impressions are called samskaras. Some impressions are supportive, some neutral, and some dense. A vibrational impression like love, peace, gratitude, bliss, or samadhi is considered supportive. An impression like brushing your teeth or urinating carries little emotional charge, little personalization, and is considered neutral.

Then there are impressions that are personalized, emotionally charged, and unresolved like fear, pain, anger, and shame—dense samskaras. It isn't that fear, pain, anger, and shame are wrong, but because this type of vibration feels "bad," you repress feeling it. You stuff it inside and refuse to bring it into the light of conscious awareness. When you do this, the energy loses momentum and becomes stuck within, obscuring the Essential Self.

When an experience and its energy impression are overly powerful, highly emotional, personalized, and unresolved, the energy becomes dense, and it limits your nervous system's ability to function at its optimal state, severely curtailing any opportunity for you to live in expansion, synchronicity, and possibility.

Resistance within you in any form is a red flag that

there is something you need to examine. The stronger your resistance is, the more deeply engrained these dense samskaras become. The degree to which you identify with, resist feeling, and personalize a circumstance is the degree to which the energy connected with that circumstance is intensified in your nervous system. The dense samskaras mask your Essential Self. They narrow your state of consciousness and cause separation to be experienced. These energies impede the flow of your life force and thus are not aligned with the soul. They are dissonant in that they hide the Essential Self. They are also the cause of scarcity and limitation, because they create barriers between you and the infinite reality and power that exists within you.

When the unresolved emotional energy of the dense samskara is resolved and freed, the memory of the event remains—but the unresolved and personalized emotional content is released, and the dysfunction and limitation it created are eliminated. When you are functioning in connection, from the place of the Essential Self, you become the Witness and no longer personalize or overly identify with an experience.

A woman I know began dating a guy who talked endlessly about his brilliant employee Sandy. He was an entrepreneur, and Sandy was crucial to the success of his business. All the time, it was, "Sandy is so smart, so brilliant, so creative, I don't know what I would do without her," "Listen to what Sandy came up with today." In his mind, he was sharing his day. But in the mind of my friend, her date's ongoing praise of Sandy aroused strong and relentless feelings of jealousy, fear of betrayal, and inadequacy. She described it as excruciating. She didn't want to come off as controlling or possessive, so she never mentioned it. But eventually it bothered her so much, she broke off the relationship.

A year later, she was on a second date with a new gentleman in a new city. They were having a great time, laughing and learning about each other. There was connection, compatibility, and good energy in the conversation. Then, as if reading off a script, he started on what seemed to be a twenty-minute monologue about his business partner, Stacy, and how smart, brilliant, and creative she was, emphasizing that his company would be nothing without her.

As the familiar words and phrases fell out of his mouth, the same difficult emotions shot up inside my acquaintance from her gut to her throat. Suddenly, she wanted nothing to do with this nice open-hearted fellow. Logically, she had no reason to feel this way. Minutes before they had been enjoying a great dinner, complete with candlelight and tasty sushi. But then when he showed her his business website and his logo was the same as the one belonging to the last guy (an orange slice, of all things), her internal reaction grew even stronger. "Sandy" was only a few letters off from "Stacy." It felt like an episode of *The Twilight Zone*. How was it possible that she found herself in practically the same scenario again? Eventually she stopped looking at the situation from the outside and turned her attention inward.

This was a samskara activation, a point of egoic personalization within her energy field. The problem wasn't Sandy or Stacy. It wasn't about either guy. *She* was the common denominator across the board, and she was being called to dissolve the imprint of an experience in which she had personalized a previous betrayal, one that was lodged as a dense energy in her vibrational sphere. With conscious, nonjudgmental observation of the experience and a willingness to face the feelings it aroused, she was able to examine her insecurity and jealousy. What she found lurking just beneath them was her own perceived unlovability and sadness and the feeling that she was never recognized for who she really was. Through a willingness to face her internal discomfort and the power of present-moment awareness, the darkness disappeared.

When you are present with an emotion without resistance or judgment, you raise its vibration through your own Beingness. Raising its vibration has the effect of allowing dense, stuck energy to vibrate at a higher frequency and regain momentum. When that dissonant energy becomes more concordant, it can become resolved and move out. It happens regardless of what you think or don't think about it, because the "I Am" energy that is your core exists beyond any logical calculation or stipulation of this physical world. Your Divine Essence is far greater than intellect. When you tap into that force through present-moment awareness, you unleash its power in your life.

> *Your Divine Essence is far greater than intellect. When you tap into that force through present-moment awareness, you unleash its power in your life*

And yet it is human nature to seek pleasure and avoid pain. Naturally, you view dense samskaras as negative, and for the most part you try to avoid them. But a dense samskara is always an entry point into a step in your evolution. Every time you are triggered, every time you feel discomfort in an interaction, there is some way for you to gain more light, more healing, more connection. Life will always bring you the circumstances you need in order to move into your highest expression. Your job is to run toward the experience.

Life will always bring you
the circumstances you need in order
to move into your highest expression.
Your job is to run toward the experience.

When I was a child, one of my favorite attractions at the London carnivals was the Hall of Mirrors. Running through one, I never tired of seeing the fantastical shapes and images reflected back at me. In one mirror, my thin squiggly legs and wobbly body supported a huge misshapen head. In another, a buglike elongated face housed beady eyes and a pencil-thin mouth. In still another, my accordion body careened off sideways at a weird angle. Some likenesses were funny, and some were distorted. A few were downright scary. Yet the origin of each was always me. Little did I know that such a fun attraction would become a powerful metaphor for my life's work.

Saints and sages throughout the ages have known that their inner state of being was mirrored back to them in all people, places, and situations. Life happened, and they were triggered, but since they understood that universal intelligence was always moving them toward their self-realization, they didn't fall prey to their reactivity. They had the greater awareness that in any moment one of two things is happening: either the wholeness of who you are is being reflected back to you, or those aspects of you that are unresolved are being revealed. Your spouse, boss, children, the news, the traffic jam, the deadlines at work—each with its traits, charms, flaws, or challenges—is serving to bring you into greater harmony with yourself.

When you start to view your life from this perspective, everything changes. Rather than running, hiding, and avoiding discomfort, you embrace it as the threshold to freedom. You end the game of projection, reflection, and judgment as you begin to see, experience, and embrace yourself in all things. What you become conscious of no longer has an unconscious hold on you. If you can allow yourself to relax and feel what needs to be felt when you are triggered, rather than shutting down, blaming, attacking, or distracting yourself, you will start to know liberation.

Being kind and compassionate is more aligned with your Essential Nature than being mean. For that reason, it has a higher vibration. Living in a peaceful, joy-filled collaborative home has a higher vibration than being in one that is filled with drama, abuse, and passive-aggressive behavior. Working in a loving, supportive environment produces a higher vibration than working in a volatile, drama-filled job where everyone is yelling. Being in a loving relationship has a higher vibration than one in which you are always fighting. Watching a funny or spiritual movie yields a higher vibration than watching a crime or horror film.

But an activity or a situation in itself is inconsequential. It is the state of being with which you perform the activity and the acceptance with which you approach life that are important. External circumstances are not the prerequisites for transformation. It is your inner connection that determines your state, your rate of vibration. There are no prerequisites for knowing God, internal or external.

Mother Teresa worked in squalor, among the poorest people on earth. Many were sick and struggling for survival. She owned practically nothing. She led the simplest of lives. But she was a spiritual giant. That didn't mean she never questioned life or struggled with emotions. But they did not dominate her experience. Her experience was one of connection and authenticity. She chose her circumstances, and they had no effect on her state of connection and her inner experience. Her alignment with her authentic self allowed her to be the custodian of her peace.

Your outer reality is always being created either consciously or unconsciously. Your vibrational resonance is always evolving. Naturally when you evolve, your choices evolve. When you change your energy, your life will change. Transformation is all about a natural acceleration of your resonance, your vibrational frequency, and that is the foundation for your evolution.

Transformation can't be forced. For example, you may think you need to renounce the world to know God. If that is in your nature, then that may be a positive for you and feel natural to you. But forced renunciation as a means to attain God simply produces more resistance. A natural increase in conscious awareness leads to a natural falling away of behaviors that are not in alignment with your soul. As your vibration increases, compassion naturally increases. The inner state frees you of all external attachments. Vibrational transformation shifts your state into a higher frequency, and when your state changes, your external life will organically find harmony and balance.

The energy of every experience you have is impressed within you. Every one. What you ingest physically, mentally, and emotionally enters your vibrational sphere. Yes, being mindful of and selecting consciously what you ingest is supportive of your vibrational state. But you can't manage every detail of your environment all the time. To attempt to do so is exhausting and inevitably impossible. So rather than hyperfocusing on your surroundings, remain anchored within, knowing that in doing so you are being supported to perpetually expand your personal frequency.

Align your vibration with the highest vibration possible by getting quiet and turning your attention inward. Make your connection to the life force that moves this universe the most important thing in your life. Be a person who lives from the inside out rather than the outside in. Cultivate your relationship with your soul, just as you would tend a beautiful garden that bears the sweetest, plumpest fruits—with scrupulous care, day by day, hour by hour. Immerse yourself in the highest vibrational frequency, and that will be reflected in your outward expression.

Make your connection to the life force that moves this universe the most important thing in your life. Be a person who lives from the inside out rather than the outside in.

Then the right food, the right clothes, the right car, the right job, the right partner, the right house will find you. You will be guided toward the manifestation of your highest good in all scenarios. When you align with your Essential Self, you will attract a vibration that resonates with yours, and you will feel that resonance in your experience. Will you still face challenges? Yes. But you will be able to sense the deeper purpose of them and reap the blessing hidden within them.

As you begin to become one with your Essential Self, the peace that is your birthright begins to permeate your experience until it becomes your constant state.

7

Awareness

ALBERT EINSTEIN, ARGUABLY THE GREATEST physicist of all time, said, "You cannot solve a problem from the same consciousness that created it. You must learn to see the world anew." And so too it is with the resolution of your core wounding. It cannot be healed by the same state of consciousness that generated it. You must raise yourself to a higher vibrational frequency to free yourself from unworthiness and unlovability. Out of fear, your wounding was created; through love, it will be dissolved.

Out of fear, your wounding was created; through love, it will be dissolved.

This dissolving occurs through the one consciousness— the one energy—that exists and moves all things, known in many traditions as God or the Divine. This energy is all that is. It is the life force of the universe, and within the individual it operates on two main levels.

On one level, it creates the action in your mind and body: the movement of your muscles, the functioning of your internal organs, the formulation of your thoughts, the movement of your lips, the growing of your hair, the flow of blood through the tiniest capillaries. It is the magnificent force that fuels the intricate workings of your eyes, allowing you to see the shapes and definition of the world around you.

On another level, it expresses itself as an evolutionary power that arises once human beings cultivate the ability to simply observe themselves without judgment. As we increase our level of awareness, this transformative power begins to move through the meridians, the vast energy network that runs throughout your entire body, opens blocked channels, resolves dense energies, and brings us into complete harmony with ourselves. It brings order out of chaos, connection out of separation, and understanding out of ignorance. Heightened awareness or conscious observation has the ability to resolve the "personalization" experience and dissolve everything that hides the Essential Self. That resolution provides access to universal love, oneness, and the experience of connection.

When you begin to cultivate greater levels of awareness, the evolutionary power within you brings everything that is unresolved inside of you to the surface to be experienced and embraced. You might find that you are very irritable and judgmental of the people around you. Even strangers annoy you. Or you may feel sadness, anger, or other pain.

The brother of a young man I know experienced a serious psychotic break that rendered him unable to communicate with others. The young man was very close to his brother, and it was extremely shocking and painful for him. It seemed as though so much was lost in the darkness. And yet, because he had started work with conscious awareness, he allowed himself to feel the tidal waves of sadness, pain, fear, and powerlessness that arose without being broken by those emotions.

He realized the best way to help his brother was to cultivate as much love as he possibly could. He knew that love was within him, on the other side of all of those layers of pain and fear. As dense emotions arose, he allowed himself to feel and release them. In the spaciousness created, his heart opened, and he gained a new empathy for those with mental illness and their families. There was a recognition of the fragility of life and the importance of living it to the fullest.

The end result was that he was internally transformed, and his life reflected it. He let go of a job that was no longer a good fit, changed cities, and began to live the way he had wanted to for some time, but had been too afraid to go for. Through this vibrational transformation, it was as if he had stepped into a new incarnation in this lifetime.

You can start vibrational transformation right now through the power of the Divine Consciousness that is within you. No matter how negatively you feel about your present situation, how much of a failure you think you are, how hopeless you've deemed yourself to be when it comes to relationships, there is that part of you, here and now, that is transcendent. It is the part of you that cannot be changed, altered, or damaged in any way.

No matter how negatively you feel about your present situation, how much of a failure you think you are, how hopeless you've deemed yourself to be when it comes to relationships, there is that part of you, here and now, that is transcendent. It is the part of you that cannot be changed, altered, or damaged in any way.

Let's say you are sharply criticized for something you said by someone close to you—a girlfriend, boyfriend, spouse, or sibling. You begin to feel deep shame, and a burning pain sets in. A few minutes after the conversation, you start to experience a familiar feeling creep over you. You've never really put words to it before, but it goes something like this: "I'm sick and tired of you calling me out. Everything I say is stupid or an embarrassment. Every time I open my mouth, you look at me like I'm some kind of loser."

This much heavy energy typically incites you to a verbal outburst or some form of striking back; you need to hurt the other as much as you are hurt. Instead of falling back into this familiar habit, employ the power of your present-moment awareness. Sit in the awareness of your feelings.

Observe your mind's endless commentary without falling prey to its unrelenting messages. If you have thoughts like, "She's always made me feel inferior. She's never had to face any real challenges. Everything she touches turns to gold. I guess Dad was right. She's too good for me. I'll never measure up," relax, take some deep breaths, and step behind everything that is playing out.

You will often find that your mind will use every resource at its disposal to achieve dissonance, to keep the internal resistance alive. But you have a choice. You can neutrally witness it all.

Resist the desire to retreat into a distraction. Leave your smartphone where it is. Step away from the alcohol. Notice the feeling in your body. Is it heavy? Is it bitter? Does it centralize around your solar plexus? Your throat? As you remain present, the lightness of Being restores momentum to heavy, stuck energy. Move into observation and feel the heaviness. Shine the light of conscious awareness on it.

At first, it can be hard to just be with yourself, as you are awash in internal discomfort. You are so trained to get somewhere, to have or create a point for everything. You are a professional human "doing," programmed for high performance, low maintenance, and fast delivery.

On top of that, from a young age, you've been taught

to see—consciously or unconsciously—sadness as weakness, stress as negative, anger as wrong, and loneliness as something to be avoided. When an uncomfortable emotion arises, like anger, your first response is to label it as unacceptable. Then you label yourself bad for feeling it. It triggers memories of your father's rage, your mother's victimhood, or your own emotional abuse, and a flood of painful samskaras are triggered. You feel as though you are drowning in quicksand.

To push away or shut down this automatic process, you reject your anger. Your rejection takes the form of stuffing it away, keeping it out of sight, and not allowing yourself to fully be in the experience of what wants to emerge from within you. You bear down, grind your teeth, slap on a happy face, and walk away. This whole chain reaction happens within a matter of seconds.

The inevitable result is that you create a life fashioned around avoiding situations that will reactivate your anger. To do so you subjugate your wants and needs, repress your desires, choke off your voice. Over time, these unresolved feelings limit your ability to interact intimately, authentically, and powerfully in the world. They block you from the richness that each day has to offer.

Emotion can be broken down into *e* + *motion*, energy in motion. High vibrational energy has momentum like a fast-moving river. Low vibrational energy is more static and dense, like molasses or wet cement. The more emotions are judged, resisted, rejected, and left unfelt, the denser that energy becomes, forming a quagmire within your vibrational system. It is not that one emotion is good and another bad. They all serve their purpose. They are all simply energy in motion. The big question is how you respond or react to that energy. Do you resist it or allow it?

The truth is, that energy doesn't want to be in you any more than you want it there. But you are unknowingly holding it in place by your refusal to feel it, thereby giving it power over you.

Any emotion that you resist or judge creates heaviness in your system. You don't resist happiness; you resist fear or sadness. You see, it is what you do with that energy that matters. Do you resist the energy of anger? Do you reject that shame? Do you think that guilt and fear are who you are and move into self-judgment?

Self-judgment creates resistance. Like a tourniquet, it blocks energy that wants to flow. Denial and repression are the tools you use to secure this tourniquet in an act of self-preservation driven by fear. This restriction of energy flow then creates your distortions, addictions, compulsions, and dependencies.

For too long, you have been frenetically racing around to mend a self that you believed was broken. You've read countless self-help books, talked through your issues numerous times, and completed a slew of workshops. But most of this was focused on changing your thoughts or building up an impressive repertoire of nice spiritual concepts. The process we are discussing is an experience of energy changes within you. It is less about knowledge and more about living in connection with your authentic self in each moment. When you start to be present for yourself and feel what there is to feel to completion, you begin to embody higher frequencies, and you become lighter, freer, and more at peace.

When you start to be present for yourself and feel what there is to feel to completion, you begin to embody higher frequencies, and you become lighter, freer, and more at peace.

To do this work, you must know that you are absolutely worthy of your own attention at any point in time. You need to learn a new way of approaching your life, one that does not depend on the highs of special events and momentary indulgences, but one that is rooted in the possibility of the present moment. It's not just the milestones of your life that count. You are more than your wedding day, your promotion, your master's degree. You learn to prioritize your well-being over your relationships, your to-do lists, your children, and your career. You come to know that how you attend to yourself here and now, including accepting your anger, self-loathing, and shame, is the key to the creation of a peace-filled existence. Everything in your present experience, including perceived challenges, heartbreak, crises, and pain, is what you need to help you come into your greatest energy expression.

Let's take a look at another example. Your sloppy roommate left a sink full of dishes again. Her perceived laziness and disregard for your shared space infuriates you. You are enraged on the inside, seething actually. Your mind goes on a rampage of blaming thoughts: "This is it. I've reached my limit. She is so lazy and irresponsible. She's a slob in the bathroom. She's inconsiderate of my wants and needs. I know she goes through my things when I'm not around, and she always needs to be reminded to pay the rent on time. I'm not her babysitter. This situation is completely unbearable. It's time to move out." The intensity of your emotional response to this one situation is so illogical and overzealous that it most likely has more to do with something that happened to you as a child than the situation at hand.

The fact is your roommate didn't wash the dishes. That is all that happened. As long as you remain impacted by the behavior of your roommate, you remain a victim in your reality.

Instead of judging the messenger (your roommate, for example), stop, slow down, take a breath, and come into present-moment awareness. Allow whatever emotion is in you to arise. Feel it. It is a samskara emerging into experience. At some point in your life, you went through a perceived trauma, and you were unable or unwilling to feel it to completion. Now it has resurfaced so that you can stop, look, feel, fully experience, and let it go. Continue to breathe and remain consciously focused on yourself. After a few moments (maybe longer), you will be able to handle the situation from a space of neutrality. You will still say what you need to say regarding housekeeping, but it won't be out of wounding, victimhood, or anger. It will be a response instead of a reaction. With practice, you will learn how to respond from a loving, nonemotional, proactive place.

Regardless of how evolved you become, people will continue to push your buttons (although your buttons will change as you release old patterns). But instead of holding someone else responsible for your feelings, you'll be able to navigate what is unfolding with grace and ease. Eventually, what once caused you to lash out or break down may not even cause you to blink twice.

And it is not just about the small scenarios you face in a day. I have met countless numbers of people who have gone through heartbreaking circumstances like unspeakable abuse, the loss of a loved one, or enduring poverty. But I have also seen them, with nonjudgmental observation and self-compassion, resolve and release their pain and go on to live empowered, happy lives. It all begins with how the individual shows up in the moment.

Consider the following story. Two mothers sit in the park carefully watching their young children play on the swings. Each sees her child fall and skin a knee. One mother runs to her child and, grabbing him by the arm, immediately begins chastising his behavior: "Why are you crying? Get tough, I didn't raise you to be a crybaby! Your behavior is embarrassing me!" This young child, already fearful from the jarring fall and painful scrape, is now further traumatized by his mother's tone, body language, and words. Children are intensely sensitive to emotional energy. He feels scared, hurt, and negated.

The other mother rushes to her child, gets down on her knees, and tends to the child with gentleness, attention, and acceptance. "That was a big fall. Tell me what hurts. What a brave boy you are. Can I kiss your knee and make it better? Do you need to be held for a bit?" This child feels safe, loved, cared for, and understood. Pretty soon he gets back up, ready to conquer the swings once again.

In every moment of life, you are both the mother and the child. When you react like the first mother judging and criticizing yourself, you rob yourself of the possibility of transformation. When you react like the second mother, you are able to meet yourself in the place of wounding and vulnerability and create the opening for a return to wholeness.

A painful situation makes you insecure or fearful. Instead of remaining present, noticing how you feel and accepting yourself, you fall prey to old story lines that trigger painful and harsh reprimands. Sometimes you simply push away your feelings. But this only guarantees that you will need to experience the same insecurity again, because your path to conscious awareness requires acceptance and nonjudgmental compassionate observation of your emotional content.

Every challenge that is met with acceptance and

compassion leads to freedom. If challenges are like gates you need to go through to get to the other side, then acceptance is the key that opens every one. Within you, there is enormous capacity for empathy and compassion. These are the highest vibrations and the most authentic human qualities.

Every challenge that is met with acceptance and compassion leads to freedom.

Facing your emotional density can be daunting and painful, even scary, but if you dive deep and suspend your fears, doubts, and self-judgments, you will embark on a magnificent path to fulfillment. Embrace yourself. Make peace with your perceived imperfections, and feel an uplifting and refreshing river of love flow through you.

8

Acceptance

ONCE YOU BECOME CONSCIOUS OF YOUR conditioning and wounding, acceptance is the next step. Acceptance is the doorway to your optimal vibrational state. Acceptance is the fastest path to oneness. It means living in harmony *with everything*—with yourself, with your reality, and with all that is unfolding. Acceptance allows energy to flow and supports the natural unfolding of life at a higher vibration, to a more evolved state and an expanded understanding.

> *Acceptance allows energy to flow and supports the natural unfolding of life at a higher vibration, to a more evolved state and an expanded understanding.*

To some of you, this kind of total acceptance sounds preposterous. Perhaps you are suffering in a loveless marriage, battling a chronic illness, enduring the daily torture of a soulless job, or drowning in debt with no viable opportunities for escape. Finding harmony within the limitations (internal or external) of your current framework can sound far-fetched. But from the standpoint of vibrational transformation, the reason you remain where you are is that you are in resistance to your reality.

What is resistance? Resistance is fear, a reluctance to feel whatever is going on inside of you. It is what locks energy in place. It stops momentum, evolution, and expansion. It is your dissatisfaction with "what is." It is your attempt to control. It is your judgment and rejection. Let's take a look at these examples.

Resistance locks energy in place. It stops momentum, evolution, and expansion.

Even though your spouse is emotionally absent, quick to criticize, and physically checked-out as a partner and parent, you feel unworthy of anything better. Your life is without flow and momentum. Over the years you've talked yourself into believing that this is all you deserve, and so you remain, falling deeper and deeper into despair with each day.

Or perhaps, with a diagnosis of a chronic illness, you are suffused with feelings of anger and unfairness. You reject "what is." You played by the rules your entire life. You gave it your all, and now you are blindsided by disease. You become rigid in the belief that you are being punished by an unjust God and refuse to look at changing your diet, drinking, exercise, or lifestyle.

Maybe you are someone who has worked for years at a job that you've grown to hate. You've been passed over time and again for promotions and now believe that your boss secretly has it in for you. You sit in judgment of everyone at work. You do the minimum amount of work to get by and are quick to fuel dissension among your coworkers. You are counting the days to retirement, thinking that once you are in a different situation, your life will magically evolve and you will rediscover some semblance of happiness and fulfillment.

Perhaps your situation is one in which there is never enough money. You can't sleep because of fears of a catastrophic end because of your financial shortfalls—bankruptcy, foreclosure, being forced out of your home. You scream at your spouse every time you see a credit-card bill arrive in the mail and secretly hate your spouse for not getting a better-paying job. You start pushing away everyone close to you. You believe no one appreciates how hard you work or cares about the out-flow of money, that your family is lazy and uncaring. By the end of the month, you are driven to sneak out to a local bar and drink until your cash runs out.

Generally, I've found that resistance manifests itself in people in two ways: attachment and aversion. Attachment is grasping at things and circumstances you believe will make you happy and end your suffering. Aversion is pushing away everything and everyone you believe is creating your unhappiness and suffering.

You can be attached to the way things are or averse to the way things are. You may want to remain twenty-one, glowing with youth and beauty, or you may hate that you are sixty and showing signs of aging. You may be attached to a certain outcome you deem "success" and averse to any sort of "failure." You can also have attachments and aversions to suffering. Some people are professional victims because of all the attention they receive each time their life falls apart. Other people want to end their lives, because they see no way to relieve themselves of their suffering. It's all resistance.

Think about how much time you spend in attachment. You are attached to how you look, how people respond to your words, and how they react when you tell them what you do for a living. You are attached to how impressive your home is, how big your bank account is, how desirable your cars are, and how enviable your Ivy League children are. You can even be attached to how many followers you have on Instagram. You may say, "Nah, I don't care about that." But imagine if eight, eighty, eight hundred, or eight thousand people stopped following you one day out of the blue. No matter how impervious you think you are to the opinions of others, you would probably experience some sort of inner letdown.

And then think about how much time you spend in aversion, pushing away the things you judge as not fitting into your idyllic vision of reality. You spend hours of your life criticizing your own body, the temple of your soul. You think, "If it could be just a little thinner here and a little bigger there, then I would be able to accept myself."

You can also be resisting your financial situation: "If I could just make another fifty grand per year, then I'd be freed up enough to focus on my spiritual growth," or, "Money isn't in my destiny. I'll always be in want." Your poor mind, locked in resistance, can't let go of all of these pushes and pulls, calculations and stipulations. There is no sense of deep calming peace, harmony, or ease.

You are also attached to certain outcomes and expectations for how things should play out for you based on your effort, as if life is a visit to the state fair: you've paid your money and won the game fair and square; now you want to choose your prize—the giant blue bear on the right. But we all know it does not always work like that. More often than not, the return on your investment doesn't come in the way you think or plan for. When you are so set on outcomes, you inevitably wind up frustrated, angry, or feeling that the universe is cruel. Either that, or you use the turn of events as an excuse to contract your energy even more, clinging faster and tighter to the illusion of control and retreating farther into the dark and lonely recesses of your separation.

Resistance is useless. Being bound by attachment and aversion is tiring and unworkable. Sometimes you feel as though you have what you want and you are happy. Then things turn sour, and you are despondent. And then someone compliments you, and you feel fabulous. But then someone publicly defames you, and you are destroyed. Then you make a lot of money, and you are happy. And then you lose it, and you are crushed. You get the picture.

How do you escape from this utterly exhausting see-saw of physical, psychological, emotional, and spiritual ups and downs? Through the restoration of your connection to your Essential Self. Only then can you begin to trust that *every experience*, no matter how challenging or difficult to embrace, is gently guiding you toward your highest expression, no matter how you see it in your limited perspective.

> *You begin to trust that every experience,*
> *no matter how challenging or difficult to*
> *embrace, is gently guiding you toward your*
> *highest expression, no matter how you see it*
> *in your limited perspective.*

I am reminded of the following ancient Chinese parable. There was a farmer who had a magnificent chestnut horse that he used to plow his fields and secure his livelihood. One day, for no apparent reason, the horse escaped and ran away. When the neighbors heard what happened, they rushed over to the farmer's house, arms in the air, yelling, "Too bad! What a terrible misfortune for you!" The farmer, seemingly unmoved by the appearance of his new lot in life, replied simply, "Maybe."

Sure enough, the very next morning, the horse came back—accompanied by three wild horses. Now the farmer, who had made a modest living before, had the potential to make much more. Upon hearing the great news, the neighbors rushed over to give their congratulations. "Such a fortuitous return!" they exclaimed. "Aren't you so lucky and favored!" The farmer once again replied simply, "Maybe."

A few days later, the son of the farmer was training one of the new horses and was bucked off, breaking his leg. "How terrible! What a bad turn of events!" said the neighbors. "Maybe," said the farmer. The following week, the military visited the town recruiting young men to go to war. Since the farmer's son had a broken leg, they passed him by. "How incredibly lucky you are!" said the neighbors. "Maybe," replied the farmer once again.

The story goes on, but the point is clear. The farmer is living his life rooted in his Essential Self. He is not captured by every single outcome. He is not making a stink at every turn of events. He lives with acceptance, having an unshakeable trust in the broader unfolding of his life. When you trust as the farmer does, it is easier to relax into the spaciousness of the present moment, where you can allow the magic of vibrational transformation to unfold.

To that end, I invite you to join me in an exercise. The purpose is to align you with what is, here and now. Find a quiet place and a comfortable chair. Maybe you can go into a lovely garden or a park where you won't be disturbed. Read the following phrases out loud, one at a time. After you say each line, inhale deeply and then exhale deeply. Allow the energy of the words to penetrate your being. When you read some of them, you may feel you want to cry, you may feel free, or you may feel nothing at all. It doesn't matter. The most important piece of this exercise is that you are fully present for yourself, coming into a conscious acceptance of your life now as the miracle it truly is.

I love and accept my anger. (inhale, exhale)

I love and accept my fear. (inhale, exhale)

I love and accept my sadness. (inhale, exhale)

I love and accept my guilt and my shame. (inhale, exhale)

I love and accept my thoughts. (inhale, exhale)

I love and accept my choices and decisions. (inhale, exhale)

I love and accept my body. (inhale, exhale)

I love and accept my ego. (inhale, exhale)

I love and accept my past. (inhale, exhale)

I love and accept every choice and every decision.
(inhale, exhale)

I love and accept my sexual energy. (inhale, exhale)

*I love and accept all that I am. I am who God made me
to be. I love and accept all that I am. I am who God
made me to be. I love and accept all that I am. I am
who God made me to be.* (inhale, exhale)

When you live in opposition to yourself here and now,
you perpetuate the collective insanity that is life lived
in its limited form. When you begin to accept who you
are, you can recognize the blessing that is flooding your
reality in each moment. In a framework of acceptance,

everything you once believed you had to overcome, fix, or change becomes a vehicle through which divine grace is channeled into this world. You see that what you were resisting about yourself was actually providing you the doorway into a bright, new reality.

I have a friend who was in a job she hated. She was an assistant to two extremely busy executives in midtown Manhattan. The issue was not that she disliked her bosses. She actually respected them a lot. Her problem was that she couldn't stand making mistakes. Her job required meticulous attention to detail, and she lived in a perpetual state of anxiety, worrying about when she would miss something crucial. She feared appearing incompetent and berated herself constantly. Even when she was home or on a day off, she was hypervigilant; she scanned her phone obsessively, feeling stressed and annoyed. On top of that, she resented the hectic pace of the city and felt that she had jumped on a treadmill that was going at high speed and had no off button.

After months of heavy resistance to herself and her life, she finally decided enough was enough. She let go completely and became willing to accept herself and all her perceived imperfections the situation had brought to the surface. No more self-recrimination. No more fear of "looking bad." No more blame. She imagined that she had three months left in the job, and in that time she let herself off the hook, completely and unreservedly. When she made a mistake, she admitted to it promptly and then basked in the uncomfortable feelings. Sometimes she was even light about it, laughing at herself. When she found herself waking up to the old barrage of negative thoughts—"I hate my life and my job, and I am useless"—she let them float by and didn't pay them any attention.

She carved out time for a yoga class or a jog by the East River. There were even a few mornings she went into the office late, giving herself much needed time to reset and recuperate. Interestingly, no one seemed to notice. She accepted her need for some downtime and permitted herself to be "imperfect" in her work environment. Amazingly, she stopped making mistakes, her bosses were happier with her performance, and she developed kind and meaningful relationships with the clients she had seen before as sources of stress. The turnaround was quick and drastic. Within just a few weeks of implementing the power of acceptance in her life, she got word that a new opportunity had opened for her in publishing, which was her true passion. Because she had been doing this internal work, she had no doubt it was the right move.

Nothing remains static. Circumstances change. Life evolves. But when we surrender our will and align with the will of the Divine, we are naturally brought into harmony with what is. The unexpected diagnosis, the heartbreak, the perceived failure, the unconscionable loss—acceptance reveals the true nature of the perceived challenges for what they truly are, an invitation to return to love and to acceptance of what is. Meeting life with acceptance has the potential to eradicate the chaos and uncertainty that define the human experience. It tames the mind and opens the higher chambers of the human heart, where trust and surrender abide. In ending your resistance to yourself and life, you are taking a vibrational leap toward the revelation of your Divine Essence.

You are coming home to the eternal you.

9

Flexibility

WHEN YOU ARE CUT OFF FROM YOUR ESSENTIAL
Self and life seems as though it is attacking you, tossing you about, and requiring so
much effort, the natural reaction is to seek some control.
You fear that if you loosen your grip, everything will fall
apart, the other shoe will most definitely drop, and you or
your loved ones will suffer.

What's your first reaction when a strong wind

blows? You stiffen and become rigid, clutching whatever will stabilize you. But a tall tree that has survived many decades of strong winds has done so because it has a certain amount of give, a flexibility in its trunk and branches. What's your first reaction when you are in the ocean and a giant wave approaches? You feverishly try to swim out of the way. If you relaxed and moved under the wave, allowing it to pass over you instead of opposing it, you probably would barely feel its force. You wouldn't end up crushed and broken on the beach.

When you relate to life too rigidly, the first hardship that blows in your direction will leave you flat. It is for that reason that the most powerful, life-giving posture you can take is one of inner flexibility.

When you relate to life too rigidly, the first hardship that blows in your direction will leave you flat.

When you are living in a created self, there is always the feeling of being out of control, because the judgment of others runs your life. You are compelled to control other people's responses to you. And then you always want their control over you to end. It's a trap, but the result is that you tend to become very rigid in your relationships with your children, with your partner, your parents, even with yourself. Things have got to be a certain way, or else you lose it.

Suppose you are the parent of a young teenage girl. You've cultivated a steadfast posture as a conservative, authoritarian mom. You know the pitfalls of adolescence that girls are susceptible to, and you've invested all your energy into instilling in your daughter the difference between right and wrong, good and bad. Despite all your years of committed focus, your teenager is becoming more and more rebellious. She is now hanging out with the wrong crowd and breaking curfew often.

Then one particularly aggravating evening, she comes home with a tattoo across her lower back. She is masterfully testing every limit you set. She is determined to become her own authentic person and end your control over her, defiantly smacking up against your vision of what she should be. With every infraction, you are quicker to explode into a seething rage, pulling the reins more tightly around her. She's constantly pissed off, sullen, and disrespectful, and you are suffering so much that now you are losing sleep and constantly fighting with your husband over the situation.

What if, instead, one morning you calmly and lovingly told your daughter that you trusted her ability to make good decisions for herself? That after sixteen years of strong influence from you and your husband, you can find peace in knowing that she has within her the intelligence, fortitude, and self-love to navigate tough situations in ways that will keep her safe? And most important, that if the time comes when she finds she is unable to make the right decision or perhaps finds she makes a decision that she regrets, you are here as her safe harbor—to love her, to listen to her, to problem solve, and to celebrate her growing independence?

When you are rooted in the Essential Self, when you have trust that everything is unfolding in divine order, the need to force the circumstances of your life into a predetermined outcome, like a square peg into a round hole, simply evaporates.

Your daughter's rebelliousness may be the gestation of a fiercely independent woman who will one day make a significant mark in her chosen profession or her community. Her desire to choose friends that are outside your comfort zone is a mark of curiosity, an attempt to explore who she wants to be, what qualities she hopes to embody.

We can't protect our kids. We can't shelter them from bad choices. We only stifle their growth and development when we try and force them into a way of being that makes *us* comfortable. Your willingness to parent from a position of inner flexibility is the ultimate gift.

Rigidity and grasping for control are not in alignment with the unrelenting flow of life, which is always moving toward expansion and evolution. Life will always challenge your preconceived notions about how things should be. This challenge is part of your evolution. When life sees rigidity, it only wants to flow, gracefully and smoothly. When life sees you grasping for control, it only wants you to be in a stream of receiving and allowing.

Life will always challenge you in order to bring you from rigidity to flexibility, from control to allowing. If you don't see this truth, your experience of friction, tension, and suffering will only intensify, causing you physical, mental, and emotional misery.

> *Life will always challenge you in order to bring you from rigidity to flexibility, from control to allowing.*

Whenever you hold hard and fast to a particular out-come or expectation, you are experiencing attachment, which naturally leads to suffering. For me, there is no set way or vision of how things should be that is worth hold-ing on to, because any fixed posture comes at the cost of my peace. I know that ultimately I am not in control; I understand Who breathes me.

I know that ultimately I am not in control;
I understand Who breathes me.

Someone who remains like flowing water, who doesn't have an attachment to set outcomes, has a greater capacity to remain peaceful and balanced. That person is like a stream that makes its way seamlessly around the rocks, logs, and bends. It may be dammed temporarily, but eventually it flows again, and all the brilliant life-forms of the greater ecosystem flourish right along with it—the fish, the algae, the plants, the frogs.

And yet there are and always will be certain people and situations that make you tense up, contract your energy, run away, or shut down completely. Perhaps it is your in-laws who make you feel like an outsider in the family; or maybe it's a colleague who undermines your every move. Maybe it's an unpaid medical bill that awakens a sleeping "fear" dragon at the bottom of your gut every time you think about it. Or maybe it's something totally inane like being coughed on while riding public transportation or a taxi driver in a foreign country who tries to rip you off. All of these scenarios set off internal reverberations that cause you to stiffen and contract your energy. They are triggers—thoughts, feelings, and events that set off instantaneous knee-jerk reactions.

Within the context of vibrational transformation, every such scenario exists to allow you to elevate your conscious awareness and energy. The more you make yourself available to your own discomfort in these moments, the more you can resolve your samskaras. If you can remain like water, you can expertly navigate yourself around the boulders and snags, knowing that each one is giving you more and more momentum for your evolution.

Let's take a look at what happens when you are triggered. It's the holidays and your three young children have had too much sugar and too little sleep. Your in-laws are staying for the weekend, and your kids are out of control. In exasperation, your father-in-law quips that if you weren't working so much and spent more time with your children, they wouldn't behave like entitled little monsters. You think to yourself that he has no idea what it takes to raise kids today—and you have three, not the single one he and your mother-in-law raised. Emotion burns hot throughout your body, and you feel your throat constrict as your cheeks flush pink. You are embarrassed, outraged, and angry. But because you want to be perceived as a "good" daughter-in-law, you say nothing, compressing your anger like a handkerchief crumpled into a small ball in your white-knuckled fist. Late at night, you lie awake and question if you are indeed guilty as charged.

When you are triggered, you almost always go into a defensive posture and inflate yourself above the hurt you're actually feeling or contract in fear. But going into any one of these modes only ensures that whatever energy was trying to flow through your experience will remain locked in place. Then a similar scenario in another interaction will produce the same vibration to give you yet another chance to experience it and release it.

The alternative is to move into a relaxed state. See the situation for what it is—an opportunity for expansion. Consciously allow your muscles to remain relaxed. Breathe and imagine a cool, gently flowing stream. Ease into the trust that everything that is brought up within you is calling for you to come into greater self-acceptance and an expanded awareness.

If you can do this in those moments when you most want to fight back, shut down, or run, you will find powerful results. You will expand your consciousness and flow with the evolution of life. Eventually, you will find that in the space you have created, you can choose how you want to respond to situations rather than react and have them control you. Your inner rigidity will melt as you put an end to your habitual reactivity.

> *Your inner rigidity will melt as you put an end to your habitual reactivity.*

Let's look at some more examples. You've spent months looking after your ailing grandfather, missing work so often you've been let go. Your finances are a disaster, and there's no paycheck in sight. You don't want anyone to know how big a financial failure you are. Your family would judge you, and your girlfriend would surely reject you. So you retreat. But then at Thanksgiving, your younger brother mentions at the dinner table that you haven't paid him back the fifty dollars he loaned you. You throb with anger and humiliation.

The reality is that your essential goodness has been fully expressed in your compassion for your grandfather, but your created self has been triggered by your family's judgment of you, which you find overwhelming. Let your mind run its course. Those thoughts are irrelevant to your vibrational transformation in this moment. Instead, consciously focus your attention on how you are feeling and the energies in your body. Where is the tension localized? Is it in your shoulders? Your lower back? Where do you feel constriction? Is it in your stomach? Your throat? If the humiliation had a color, what would it look like? Let that wave roll over you. Breathe and recognize the discomfort as an opportunity to come into greater transformation.

Five years after a long contentious divorce, you spy your ex at a restaurant one evening. Even after all this time, your stomach still turns inside out and upside down, and you begin to feel sick. Adrenaline swamps your nervous system. Your heart begins to race, as all the old feelings of anger and betrayal suffuse your being. And then, in an instant, you feel the sting of tears as you are awash in the belief that, ultimately, you weren't good enough for him. Instead of leaving your friends and ruining a beautiful night, take an internal step back and watch yourself in your discomfort. Allow the feelings to bubble up within you. Breathe deeply. Stay rooted in your Essential Self, as whatever needs to be felt is embraced and released.

Becoming aware when you are being triggered allows you to choose inner flexibility. Lean into the totality of your experience. Release whatever emotional density is being revealed. Allow it to leave. Your circumstances, no matter how uncomfortable, are no mistake. The Divine is giving you the chance to consciously feel to completion whatever heavy, dense energies are within you, so that you can move into liberation. You may eventually make changes to improve your situation, but when you do so, it will be from a place of higher vibration, inner resolution, and responsiveness.

When you disrupt your reactive patterns by cultivating inner flexibility, you can approach life from a place of neutral observation. Then, when you act from a place of connection and flow rather than contraction and ego, your actions will have a greater, more aligned effect.

Are you starting to see the connection between triggers, acceptance, flexibility, and your evolution? There is a universal energy called shakti, which resides within you, powering your every breath. There is a life force energy, called prana, that moves you. It is always wanting naturally to flow upward into a higher, more expanded state. It is pushing you toward the experience of your Essential Self. But your resistance, your need to control, and your inflexibility thwart its movements, impede its momentum, and cause you to remain separate and in suffering. Acceptance and flexibility restore the natural flow of shakti and prana. They bring peace and end suffering. They accelerate your expansion and evolution.

It's interesting how we think about things in our lives as either negative or positive. Being stressed, fearful, ill, alone, or low on cash are all "negative" experiences to be avoided. Being in a relationship, sipping a cocktail on the beach in Tahiti, being perfectly fit and healthy, or having a prestigious high-paying job are all "positive" experiences to be pursued. You think being without any pressure or fear is good, while responsibilities are heavy and cumbersome. But all of these judgments are just the result of separation, false perceptions, and social programming.

You perceive everything not from a place of neutral expansion, but from your conditioned stance, your ego. The outcome is that you wind up in constant resistance to life, because it does not show up in a way that keeps you comfortable in your conditioning.

But that is not its job. The job of life is to bring you

into the fullness of your Essential Self. No matter how unexpected or even how painful your life is right now, it is only showing up to bring you into a more expanded state of being.

This happens on macro and micro levels. A country elects a president, and you love or hate him. He must run the business of the country, but from a larger perspective he is playing the role of bringing into conscious awareness all that is unresolved in the country's people—the bigotry, hatred, anger, and fear. This is part of the group expansion. On a personal level, your mother gets into your business, and it brings up old feelings of being trapped and scrutinized. Your partner unwittingly triggers your insecurities about your lovability. Your dear friend is given a terminal diagnosis, and it brings up sadness, helplessness, desolation, and the fear of your own death. Through the limited perspective of your conditioning, these situations are "bad." But through the perspective of vibrational expansion, all of these individuals and energies are giving you the chance to bring that which is unconscious into conscious awareness, that which is unresolved into resolution.

The same idea applies to stress. You are conditioned to see stress as bad, disruptive of your life and destructive to your health. It is something to be avoided. But feeling stressed is quite simply your natural response to challenging circumstances; it is your ability to adapt to change. That's it. It's not, as the media would have you believe, a scary monster out to snatch your life. It's the ebb and flow, the inhale and exhale of existence itself. If you could break out of your conditioning about stress, you would be able to see it as a blessing rather than evil. Studies have shown that people who think stress is a bad thing were the ones who were negatively affected by it and that a moderate amount of stress can actually be beneficial to neural functioning and learning. It is your conditioned perception of the experience of stress that is always more detrimental to your well-being than any experience itself.

Your triggers are your chance to wake up and become more consciously aware. The cultivation of inner flexibility allows them to be brought to resolution. They are your liberation, if you allow them to be.

10

Consciousness at Thirty-Three Thousand Feet

A GOOD PORTION OF YOUR MENTAL ENERGY IS involved in dealing with what has been done to you, the wrongs that have taken place in your life and the world, the times you were victimized, taken for granted, unappreciated, and abused. Much of your remaining energy is taken up with your regrets and shame, worrying about the wrongs you committed and how and when you may be found out.

This is because when you live in a created self, you personalize everything. Your life is lived through the lens of your ego. Your reality is good or bad personally, right or wrong morally, left or right politically, true or false philosophically. It is a set of egoic stances. And life is always happening *to you*. You feel as though you are the sum total of what other people and outside forces have done to you or how you have been judged and labeled.

> *When you live in a created self,*
> *you personalize everything.*

But the Essential Self has a much broader and more inclusive view. It is conscious awareness at thirty-three thousand feet. When you take off in an airplane, you can see the topography of the land, the symmetry of the lush emerald fields, the pattern of the red and brown rooftops, the tall buildings reflecting light like giant mirrors. You can see that it makes sense for one road to intersect another and why there is a certain infrastructure around major highways. You don't ever see that from the ground.

From the perspective of the highest understanding of your soul, life is a neutrally unfolding expansion in which everything is happening in perfect divine order. In every seemingly inconsequential moment of every seemingly inconsequential day, divine grace is moving you toward greater evolution. Your limited perspective might only see a stop sign or a pothole and judge it as annoying or intolerable, but your Essential Self, which is one with the Divine, is tapped into a greater consciousness, one that trusts and allows the highest outcome to emerge.

*From the perspective of the
highest understanding of your soul,
life is a neutrally unfolding expansion
in which everything is happening
in perfect divine order.*

Everything is a part of this awakening: the love and the marriage proposal, the victimization, the lack of appreciation, the birth, the death, the abuse—every single encounter. It is also the boredom, the addiction, the long commute, the early morning walks in the park, the party on the deck, the overtime at work. The feeling of separation and the feeling of connection. If you could live with the conscious awareness of viewing the world at thirty-three thousand feet, you would see that everything that is occurring is bringing you to a complete state of realization, your full enlightenment. It is grace, the conscious recognition that there is perfection at work in everything. Every experience has been created for the purpose of awakening you.

> *Every experience has been created for the*
> *purpose of awakening you.*

Realize that this entire reality has been supporting your expansion. Let go of the past, the victimhood, and the story, because the truth is that you are not your story. You are not your pain. You are not your position. You must learn to trust life and let go of all that is veiling your Essential Self. You must learn to surrender, knowing that in the act of surrendering you are letting go of the resistance to what is unfolding right now. In that trust, there is freedom.

*Learn to surrender, knowing that in the act
of surrendering you are letting go of the
resistance to what is unfolding right now.
In that trust, there is freedom.*

I know it is difficult to recognize that a situation that
made you a victim, that wounded you, is also an opportunity. But as long as you externalize the problem, you can't
receive the solution. Holding fast to the blame and anger
against your parent, friend, boss, or partner doesn't allow
resolution to occur in your own being. You must shift into
the perspective that, in the most powerful experiences of
your life, you are given the opportunity for the expansion
of *your* consciousness. Over time, you are able to see how
these experiences served *your* evolution. In short, everything in your life has happened for *you*. You are repeatedly
being shown the crack that is the opening for grace. But
you must be willing to look directly at it and feel it, turning victimhood into empowerment.

Let's put this into practice. First, take a minute to
think about something that you have trouble letting go
of. Then, when you are ready, take yourself through the
following set of questions. Remember, you are viewing
this interaction from thirty-three thousand feet above.

What emotions did my experience produce: sadness, anger, shame, fear?

What qualities, characteristics, or traits did I take on because of the experience?

Who am I today because of it?

How has it shaped my experience of life?

Has the story of my wounding been exaggerated by my trapped emotions?

What was the purpose of the experience?

Reason, inquiry, and understanding are the lights that allow you to let go of reactivity and bring you into personal accountability, honesty, clarity, and resolution. There was suffering—but the mind tends to exaggerate the experience and then fear creates a distortion. The mind interprets that distortion as reality and creates your story. The turnaround you create in the mind can give you clarity on what is actually true for you. And then you can release the energy of fear through vibrational transformation. The alternative is continuing to live in an unfair reality where God is unjust and suffering is the best you can hope for.

One of my best friends is gay. When he came out to his family, he was disowned. His mother, with whom he had been close, told him that, as far as she was concerned, he was dead. She never again spoke to him. This was unbearably painful to him. He wondered, "How could this happen to me?" But then he realized that, for the first time in his life, he was no longer in the grip of conditioning. He could be fully himself. He no longer had to live to please his family, to win their love and approval, and he could create the life that was most authentic for him. He went on to build a more successful and fulfilled life than he previously could have imagined. His family's rejection of him became the jumping-off point for his greatest expansion. He told me that what had happened with his family was grace. He said that it had made him understand suffering of others in a way that most people never will. It brought out the deepest compassion in him.

Everything you experience serves a purpose. It feels so difficult because it is so personal, so hurtful. But you have the power to transform your relationship to it.

How do you accept trauma, rejection, and abandonment as part of your evolution? It's helpful, in a difficult situation, to see not just the negative—but both the negative *and* the positive. Most people compartmentalize experiences as either good or bad, but doing so only creates rigid boundaries that further limit us. Perceived negative life experiences create positive attributes in you that would not have been present otherwise. Life experiences shape you, but do not have to define you. Who you are is defined by the Divine.

One who has experienced abuse is better able to have compassion for those who have been abused. Those who have battled cancer can hold a loving space for those who are still in the midst of that fight.

Yes, sometimes people get stuck in repetitive traumatic loops, but for most, suffering becomes an entry point for compassion and serves to redirect people toward love. There is grace in this—and grace always allows for expansion, if you are open to it.

The next step toward ending your sense of being victimized is letting go of any harmful incidents and all that is associated with them vibrationally. This is what I call "vibrational forgiveness," and it starts with just becoming aware of the source of the abuse or transgression in each case. Context creates compassion. How were the offenders raised? What suffering did they endure? Open yourself to understand the context. Sometimes, when it is really difficult to let go, it helps to envision a transgressor as a poor helpless child in pain. Then, through even the slightest compassion conjured through that visualization, there is a softening of the need to hold on to the emotion, the energy, the story. It absolutely does not mean that what they did was innocent. It just creates an opening for new energy to become associated with the incidents for *you*. This is not about the perpetrators. This is about *your* reaching an experience of samadhi, oneness.

Oneness is an all-inclusive state of experience in which all things are encompassed as a part of you; there is no transgressor, and therefore there can be no transgression. Think about all the people in your life whom you blame for the things that you believe have gone wrong—the heartbreak, the divorce, the criticism, the financial shortcomings. What if all of this—regardless of how you perceived it in the moment—was nothing more than a call to return to love? In fact, in the presence of love, none of these events would have affected you in the way they did. I know that for many of you this is a challenging truth to grasp. However, in the absence of the willingness to grasp it, one can never truly be free.

Jesus illustrated this most poignantly when, on the cross, he asked God's forgiveness of those who crucified him: "Father, forgive them, for they know not what they do" (Luke 23:34). At the level of expanded experience rooted in the Essential Self, there is a conscious acknowledgment that everything originates from the Divine, and as a result there is nothing and no one to blame or forgive. Everything is serving to move you to greater levels of harmony. Vibrational forgiveness is simply the act of freeing ourselves from the memory of trauma by having the courage to turn and face the totality of the experience that we were once unable to process.

A common misperception states that, if everything originates from the Divine, then the Divine must have a preference *for or against* whatever is unfolding. If there is love, then there must be hate. If good exists, then so must evil. In the face of justice, surely injustice exists as well. All of these are limited perceptions formed at the level of consciousness from which they are observed. However, being operates at the level of choiceless awareness. Preference is an egoic phenomenon. When you have a preference, an attraction or an aversion toward something, that's a clear indication that you are operating from your ego or the created self. Being is love and has no preference.

When I experienced the Divine on that fateful night in 2003, I experienced an all-inclusive totality that embraces both the conscious and the unconscious equally. The Divine is neither for nor against anything. This truth means that the pure potential of the Divine is being interpreted by human beings either consciously, bringing about benevolent outcomes that are aligned with love or that further our experience of oneness, or unconsciously through fear, exacerbating the collective wounding to the degree that it expresses itself as atrocities, genocide, or global inequality, to name just a few.

The Divine isn't the source of every malady or challenge that we face. *We are.* The longer we live in resistance to what is unfolding in our lives, feeling victimized while looking for someone or something to blame, we suffer.

The Divine is pure potential that is being interpreted either with clarity, meaning that it shines through for the benefit of the world, or through a distortion, pain, or wound, which automatically separates and fragments us, allowing individuals or groups to perpetuate the infliction of pain and hatred on others. You can live with impartiality, being neither for nor against.

Jesus, whose awareness was complete, recognized that his persecutors were operating from an entirely different level of consciousness than his. This allowed him to accept everything—even his crucifixion—as the will of his divine Father.

Jesus said, "Father, forgive them." This is an important point. Jesus's human part is not forgiving them. It is the Being part, the Father part of Jesus, that is forgiving. Resolution cannot come on an egoic level. Resolution is an act of grace and therefore can only be found in the Divine, on the level of the Essential Self. An ego cannot forgive another ego. Only a soul can embrace another in compassion and find vibrational resolution.

Through grace, resolution is possible. A new relationship with the trauma can ensue, and the trauma can be transformed. But very often people who are heavily identified with suffering can't find freedom from it. The freedom lies in handing it over to the Divine in a state of profound vulnerability. Asking the Divine for resolution is the ultimate act of surrender.

> *Asking the Divine for resolution is the*
> *ultimate act of surrender.*

There was a rough period during my late teenage years when my family was in crisis. My parents' relationship had broken apart for a time. I was scared, and I didn't want to feel my own grief, let alone the river of sadness and hurt between my parents—a rush of charged emotion I couldn't avoid because of the empathic energy gift that is my legacy. In an attempt to escape my own pain and fear, I began drinking heavily and using drugs. I was in deep resistance to myself and life. I wanted to control my parents' choices. More than anything I wanted us to be a normal, loving family, but nothing I did could change what was unfolding.

My father was an easy target for my own frustration. In my eyes, he was incapable of showing up as a responsible, reliable source of strength and support. No matter the circumstances, he was always preoccupied with having a good time while chasing the next big payday—a payday that never materialized. My mother, on the other hand, was my rock. Through sheer determination to provide, she gave me the stability of a loving home and her consistent presence, all the while working to provide a financial foundation for our family. Not knowing the deeper intricacies that contributed to my parents' behaviors, in my immaturity it was so easy to blame my dad for his perceived shortcomings.

Rebelling and numbing the pain seemed to be the easiest way to navigate those emotionally challenging times, as my family went through a necessary period of upheaval. There were many occasions during that time when I was incredibly harsh toward my father. I wanted to hurt him as much as he had hurt my mother and me.

As I grew older, my problem with the kind of man my father was increased. At the height of my pain, I vowed that one day I would be financially successful enough to provide for my mother, believing that in some way this would free her of the pain that I could feel emanating from her.

On Father's Day, while I was on retreat at the ashram, I felt an overwhelming need to call my father. Hours, days, and weeks of sitting in the discomfort of my own resistance to the many ways that life had seemingly shortchanged me had finally given me access to the pain that I had falsely believed had been created by my father. I needed to connect with him. I needed to tell him how much I loved him and how sorry I was for any distress I had caused. When I finished, the line was unexpectedly silent. And then I heard him say quietly, "I was only ever playing the role that you needed me to play for you." I could cry just thinking about the grace that was flowing through the phone line, streaming across the country and into my heart with those words. What my father was acknowledging is the profound understanding that all the people in your life—those who love you, hate you, cheat on you, steal from you, and bless you—are only playing their crucial role in your expansion. Everyone and every situation is the catalyst for transformation and the blessing of awakening.

You have been told you have done wrong, and others have wronged you. But the reality is that life is always playing out in the highest way for all involved to learn and expand into who they are meant to be. When you operate with this awareness, it is easier to not get caught up in emotional entanglements or conflicts. There is no greater way to experience day-to-day interactions than from a place of love and connection to your Essential Self.

Life is always playing out in the highest way for all involved to learn and expand into who they are meant to be.

Don't get me wrong. I am not excusing or condoning anyone's bad behavior. I am saying that the removal of the judgment allows you to experience the behavior for what it truly is—a distortion in that individual's lens of perception that amplifies and projects fear and pain out into the world rather than oneness and harmony. When behavior sends out energy, it will have an effect. Create a specific energy and give it momentum, and that energy will move out into this world and influence what it comes into contact with. My intention is simply to awaken conscious awareness of the deeper reality that exists.

When you are watching a movie, regardless of how perfectly or terribly it is scripted, acted, or directed, you don't demand an apology from the writers, actors, or director. In the same way, if you are simply witnessing your own life connected to your Essential Self, you are no longer personalizing every glance, every gesture, or perceived mistake as "for" or "against" you. You are no longer compelled to demand an apology for how your life works out.

With this perspective, why require forgiveness from the "actors" who were only ever playing the roles you needed them to, or from the "producer," the Divine Intelligence that laid out your life to unfold in complete perfection?

Why are you still holding people's inability to meet you in an expanded state of awareness against them?

Why hold your ex-husband hostage for playing the Oscar-nominated role of the philandering, unscrupulous jerk? Why demand that your self-centered, narcissistic boss acknowledge you for your hard work and dedication? Not everyone has the same capacity to perceive reality in the way that you do, yet you continue to expect them to show up differently, which is impossible.

Consider that guy you dated who is a serial cheater— can you keep holding him responsible for his emotional unavailability, when painful unpredictability defined his childhood and he lacked the tools to deal with it? What about your parents, who originated within an entirely different generation? Can you really continue to hold them in contempt for their perceived limitations?

Again, I am not suggesting you hang on to destructive relationships or dismiss the fact you were abused. I am simply asking you to raise your consciousness with regard to your perceived hurts, so that they can no longer control you on an unconscious level, where, left unaddressed, they silently wreak havoc in your life.

As you are elevated to higher energy levels, you have the opportunity to release and resolve the deepest layers of any dense energy—of any betrayal or upset you are still holding on to and refusing to let go. You can transform your prior grievances and find gratitude for the role everyone has played so well for you—thanking all of your former transgressors for "giving" you such profound opportunities for expansion.

When you see life from thirty-three thousand feet, you can step completely out of the cycle of shame, blame, and guilt. You can come into a pure, high vibration of love and gratitude, where you allow your full light to shine through and generate the greatest possibilities for everyone on this planet.

There is a singular purpose to everything: evolution. More bliss. More consciousness. More connection. And so too it is with you, being one with the Divine, the life force of the universe. You are always on the threshold of more. Life is supporting you, and you are infinitely loved in each and every moment.

There is a singular purpose to everything: evolution.

The Divine didn't get it wrong when it made you. The Divine didn't get it wrong when you experienced perceived harms, when you forgot your Essential Self.

Just as it didn't get it wrong when you felt love or peace or when you felt stress or fear.

Trust it. Allow it. Accept it, and begin to taste the samadhi that is possible for you.

It is all perfection moving into a greater experience of perfection.

11

The Shift

W HEN WAS THE LAST TIME YOU GOT LOST IN A
good book? Or baked an apple pie "for no
reason" and then savored each hot sweet
bite? Or spent time in nature . . . Or sat down at the
piano . . . Or played racquetball . . . Or consciously did
whatever it is that makes you feel a sense of connection
and pleasure? I hope it was very recently. But if not, you
are not alone.

In all likelihood, you were not conditioned to make your well-being a priority, to extend love and respect to yourself. In fact, you probably learned the opposite. You may have learned to give all your love and kindness to others, making their happiness the barometer of how worthy you were of that same love and kindness. You may have learned it is "selfish" to try to meet your own physical and emotional needs. Perhaps you were unofficially assigned the role of emotional caretaker to dysfunctional parents at a young age. Or maybe you learned to sacrifice your needs just to keep a sense of normalcy within your family unit. Maybe you were trained to achieve in order to feel acknowledged or taught that love means rescuing others from their demons. Maybe you absorbed the programming that a relationship means "I belong to you and you belong to me," regardless of whether the parties feel a sense of wholeness and contentment within themselves.

However you were programmed to experience love, you are now at a point where you are ready for the highest understanding of it: the fundamental truth that love originates within you. Although the outside world or that special someone can trigger the experience, it can never be its source.

Love is not about having, needing, controlling, achieving, or getting something. It is about the direct experience of the Essential Self. When you access that internal reservoir, it can extend outward to others with simplicity, compassion, and warmth. People will feel love from you because that is the energy radiating from your authentic self, which has been liberated through your self-acceptance, the resolution of your emotional density, and your expanded awareness.

When you seek outwardly to fill your inner void, you never really feel fulfilled. Either you make someone else the source of the love you crave (codependency), or you blame someone or something else for the things you feel your life is lacking (victimhood). In either scenario, you've taken an internal experience, like the experience of love or peace, and externalized it, effectively assigning others control over your life. You are back where you started, looking for love and completion in all the wrong places.

Take back your power, own your singular experience of life, and open yourself to the love within. When you take responsibility for how you show up in the present moment, you step into your sovereignty as an empowered, integrated, divinely connected human being walking this earth. When you can meet yourself without expectation and just relax into who you are here and now, others are freed to do the same thing.

*When you can meet yourself without
expectation and just relax into who you are
here and now, others are freed to do the
same thing.*

In truth, love is not so much a feeling or emotion, but rather a fundamental experience of reality. To love is to "be with" life—unconditionally. Everything else is a distortion projected onto life as a result of your inner separation. The more you are able to "be with" your moment-to-moment experience, embracing everything you have deemed unlovable, the freer you are. The less you are able to "be with" life, the more you are resisting life and the unresolved aspects of yourself.

Living in your created self, you have been almost completely immersed in reactivity and resistance. Spirituality is about dying unto oneself—the death of the psychological, created, egoic self. What is left is love, which is an expansive experience of neutrality, openness, and spaciousness. In neutrality, you don't need to lash out and react. You can pay attention to what is happening in the present moment within you, without judgment. You can embrace what you find internally in relation to what is happening externally. You can sit in neutrality with the anger, the sadness, and the fear. In "being with" life, you dissolve the distortion.

More often than not, we strive to create better versions of our future selves, to "improve" ourselves in order to feel loved and accepted by others. But the truth is, universal love is already within you, right now, as you are. These are not just words. This is the reality of you.

> *Universal love is already within you, right now, as you are. These are not just words. This is the reality of you.*

When you fully embrace this reality, you will be able to be a living, breathing beacon of divine energy. People will relax around you and feel comfortable and safe in your presence. Your relationships will be infused with the energy of bliss and connection, because it is what you will have been revealing within. Your energy will no longer be wasted on trying to leech love from people or to appear "more than" or "less than" you are. As you come to align with the love within you, you will start to be at peace with yourself and with everyone in your life.

You will be anchored from the inside, so that no matter what is going on around you—no matter who is in the hospital, who walked out on you, or who didn't text back—you will shine.

As you come to align with the love within you, you will start to be at peace with yourself and with everyone in your life.

As you move from resistance, attachment, and aversion into acceptance, love, and connection, you will be transformed. But it is important to reiterate that transformation is not about becoming someone else. It is *not* about replacing the created self with a nicer, more spiritual, more loving version of a created self. Transformation is about unveiling the light within—it is an act of illumination and enlightenment. When you remember your Essential Self, love is revealed. And then regardless of what is unfolding in your life, it too reveals itself as love. It is about creating a new relationship with you and your world—it is oneness.

*When you remember your Essential Self,
love is revealed. And then regardless of
what is unfolding in your life, it too
reveals itself as love.*

Your life, like all of creation, is constantly evolving. Nothing in the natural world remains static. Only humans fight relentlessly for things to stay the same, convinced that the way it is is the best it can be. We hold on steadfastly to experiences, ways of being, and beliefs that do not serve our well-being.

Through fear, lack of trust, and conditioning, you form all sorts of egoic attachments, and you try to control everything. But to live from the profound state of transformation, you must release these attachments and create a new relationship with all aspects of life: your society, your family, your friends, and especially yourself—your emotions, thoughts, beliefs, concepts, and understandings.

Consider your relationship to your emotions. Let's say you are watching the news and see something that brings up sadness and fear within you. Instead of remaining rooted in your Essential Self, accepting the sadness and fear with love as tools that will bring you to a greater level of conscious awareness, you become the feelings. They take control. A bit later, when a friend calls you inviting you to dinner, you decline because you are feeling low, tired, and down. As soon as an emotion takes you captive and its energy becomes stuck, you are cut off from the flow of life—a flow that wants to move you forward. And you are then blocked from any inspiration that could move you toward meaningful, constructive action.

You get a call from work that they need a proposal from you right away. You feel stress, since you are currently at the mall buying your child art supplies for a school project that is due. As you imagine your boss tapping his pen impatiently, you start to feel very anxious. In just a few short moments after hanging up the phone, you are not just feeling unease—you have morphed into a swirling, tangled, chaotic ball of distress, shoving people out of your way, being impatient with your child, and then putting off the treat the two of you were going to share.

Instead of remaining firmly rooted in your Essential Self, allowing the anxiety to rise within you, trusting that whatever comes your way you can handle, and stepping up to the challenge, you became your feeling, and then your inner experience gets mirrored back to you. If you can simply be aware that this is happening, if you can relax into the discomfort, you can pull yourself out of the limited identification; you can restore the conscious awareness of the Observer, the Essential Self.

The higher your level of conscious awareness when you are in the heat of the moment, the more you can respond and not react. When you can unveil the one watching, you are no longer captured by or identified with the thought, the emotion that is being experienced. From this grounded platform of foundational strength, all the different aspects of your being are part of your unified experience. And you can live in complete acceptance of all of it. That shift allows life to be lived in connection.

Now consider the mind. The mind is always changing, fantasizing, and judging. It works overtime to relieve its pain and wounding. It is always trying to make you acceptable and lovable. There might be times you deem yourself crazy, because your mind is creating crazy thoughts. You are thinking about a certain outcome that you want to come to pass—a ring on your finger, money in the bank. Your mind is obsessing about it constantly. Instead of stepping back and observing your mind as it tries as hard as it can to bring about the desired outcome, you become the entanglement. The obsession takes over, leaking now into your emotions and relationships. Comparing yourself to others, you start to feel that life isn't fair. "How come everyone else seems to be finding love and having babies?" "How come everyone else seems to be able to make money?" Your experience is fraught with anxiety and dissatisfaction.

If you had been able to remain as the Observer of your mind, you could watch it weave its fantasies without losing yourself in them. You could once again soften and relax in harmony because you know your Essential Self. You could trust in the timing and order of the universe because it is one with the Divine. That shift into observation takes the energy out of the obsession.

When you create a new relationship with your mind, recognizing that it is a psychic instrument whose job it is to think, identify, quantify, decide, and relate, then you can withdraw your identification with the thoughts and observe them dispassionately. Then you can say, "Look at that mind creating so many thoughts, so many good and bad, happy and sad, creative and destructive thoughts. That's its job. I will observe them and not become them." This shift allows a new and peaceful relationship with your mind.

Now let's look at the relationship you have with people. You want them to love you, accept you, honor and respect you. You want them to bestow worth upon you.

But what if you were to shift this relationship? What if you stopped seeing them as sources of approval or disapproval, love or rejection? What if you could simply live in the present moment, observing what you are doing, and decide that God made you as a unique vehicle to express God's intelligence and energy in this world? How would that shift your interactions, your feelings of unworthiness, your ability to step into your uniqueness and create from that place?

Let's look at your relationship to life. You spend the vast majority of your time resisting "what is." You spend the majority of your time in attachment and aversion— pushing, pulling, grasping, and struggling. What if you shifted your relationship with life and allowed life to unfold in its own time? What if you accepted "what is" and moved into the flow and momentum that is already within you?

And what about the relationship you currently have with yourself? You live in separation, struggle, and limitation. Interior battles rage. Shame and guilt appear. Victimhood arises. What if you shifted this relationship? What if you finally realized that everything that has happened in your life has happened in service to your expansion and evolution? Now you can see the past in a different light and move into a future of possibilities.

You can't escape yourself, no matter how hard you try. The only option is to end your resistance—to move from attachment, aversion, and control into allowing, acceptance, and flow. If it hurts when you put your hand on a hot stove, stop putting your hand on a hot stove. If your suffering is caused by resistance, stop resisting. When you end resistance, life becomes easier and more peaceful; it flows.

Throughout my life there were times that the thought of letting go evoked deep feelings of pain and fear. One of my greatest hidden fears was that, as I evolved into higher states of consciousness, fulfilling my own Essential Nature, I would have to let go of people who couldn't evolve alongside me. I would imagine a life without those that I had come to love deeply—my wife, my children, my parents. I was attached. There was such a deep sadness at my core.

But I came to know that by sitting in the sadness rather than being averse to the discomfort, the perfect outcome always comes into being. To this day that looks to me like the ultimate realization: there is a perfection to the people who have been placed around you. They don't have to be anything other than who they are. Everyone is on their own perfect evolutionary path. My family now serves as a loving tether to a reality that once felt foreign to me. Family life is not something I need to leave behind; indeed, it is something that continues to flow as I increase my capacity to accept and allow.

Last, let's consider your relationship to your purpose. Is your purpose to become rich, famous, powerful, successful, smarter, wiser, or more enlightened—something other than what you currently are? Something outwardly focused, seeking fulfillment? Maybe a better parent, a better lover, a better employee, a better devotee? What if you changed your relationship to "purpose"? You believe that if you become someone "better"—someone more "acceptable"—you will have achieved your purpose. You will be happy. But what if your purpose is to know your Essential Self?

What about your relationship to time? Here what is needed is a shift into what I call *expanded mindfulness*, which is simply the ability to gently press the brakes and slow down into the spaciousness of the present moment. Power only exists in the now. The past and the future hold no power for transformation. The past is mostly unresolved stories, unworthiness, and victimhood. The future is mostly fear and worry. The present moment is where you can shine the light of your consciousness on that which was unconscious, so that you are no longer held captive by your reactions. The present moment is the resting place of the Essential Self.

Power only exists in the now. The past and the future hold no power for transformation.

Shifting your relationships with your mind, other people, life, yourself, your purpose, and ultimately time moves you in the direction of ease, peace, oneness, and acceptance. The shift is a gentle adjustment, a loosening of the fist that grips. Then the boundaries, the separation, and the aversions can dissolve, and you can be open to the infinite.

The body, mind, and emotions are small waves in an infinite ocean. The infinite ocean is the Essential Self, encompassing everything in its expanse and depths. To identify with the Essential Self in all circumstances at all times is to know peace. That is bliss, abundance, well-being, love, and freedom.

Knowing the Essential Self is fulfillment. It is samadhi.

12

Enter the Heart

THE RESULT OF ACCEPTANCE AND VIBRATIONAL transformation is not that you become a doormat. It is not an excuse to do nothing about your situation, whether it is an abusive relationship, a job that is unsupportive, or a dear family member who is taking advantage of your good heart and pocketbook. Quite the opposite, vibrational transformation sets the stage for empowered, inspired, dynamic action.

Vibrational transformation sets the stage for empowered, inspired, dynamic action.

When you end your resistance to "what is," you are freed from attachment and aversion. The mind relaxes. You move away from the intellect's sharp problem-solving mode and into a deeper, softer realm of intuitive feeling. There is a sense of relief. Equilibrium is established in your being, and your heart blossoms like a lotus flower. And this aligned, high-vibrational energy then informs your decisions. Your most powerful expression in the world is possible when it arises from this realm of warmth and tenderness.

When I left my family and moved from London to the United States with only my small savings, it was because I was finally honest with myself and listening to my heart. I had gone through great pain and grappled internally to accept who I was and what I had come to share with the world. Though, logically, it may have made more sense to remain in London, secure a steady income through one of the family businesses, and pass that on to my children, I knew in my heart that the imprint I was meant to leave on this world was one of love and enlightenment. With that knowing as my signpost, I gracefully walked into the life that I lead today, a life that is resonant with my soul.

Your heart is also what allows you to embrace the deepest, darkest parts of your created self and bring them into resolution. These deepest, darkest parts of yourself are usually found cloaked in the guises of your subpersonalities. Subpersonalities are egoic adaptations that help you navigate the world—coping mechanisms that protect you from feeling your perceived lack of worth and lovability. They emerge when repressed trauma arises. The intensity of your wounding keeps them in place. When you find yourself challenged, judged, threatened, or in a situation where the ego feels in danger, a subpersonality asserts itself. It is an egoic survival response.

Your heart is also what allows you to embrace the deepest, darkest parts of your created self and bring them into resolution.

Let's say you are at work and your boss excludes you from a meeting. You take it personally. You feel undervalued, unappreciated. An overwhelming feeling of injustice arises in you and you flush red with anger. You walk over to his executive assistant and explode in a rage, not even realizing that you are out of control. When you come back from this expression of the subpersonality responsible for the anger and rage, you feel shame and guilt—and deep fear of retribution. You stuff it all away because it's too painful to look at. Often, when you are experiencing one of your subpersonalities and engaged in its behavior, the pain has taken over and you are not aware that you are acting out in real time.

Someone recently told me about a run-in she had with a friend at a wedding. A woman was not seated where she wanted. She felt left out and targeted, and a deep-seated subpersonality became activated. She became enraged and went off on a shocking verbal tirade that made her almost unrecognizable. This happens. Sometimes people start to behave in ways you would never suspect, because they have become egically threatened, sometimes in the most unlikely of situations. In more superstitious times, it was almost like another entity had entered their body. A person you love might suddenly start acting like someone you don't recognize: angry, sad, fearful, judgmental. He or she might lash out or run away.

The average person has between eight and twelve subpersonalities hiding inside, ready to jump out to protect the created self. These subpersonalities might take certain archetypal shapes such as the rebel, the tyrant, the mother, the innocent, the white knight, the saboteur, or the guardian, just to name a few. The reason that "spiritual" people have so much difficulty dealing with these parts of themselves is because they have been trained to believe they are unacceptable. Who wants to admit that they are on occasion powerless over their mind and body? It is only through complete, loving, heart-centered acceptance and inclusion that you can integrate the pain that created the subpersonality. When the pain is gone, the subpersonality collapses upon itself.

The path of enlightenment requires nurturing those immature aspects of yourself and coming to the understanding that every single aspect of the self is necessary in its greater evolution. With this inclusivity, you resolve the fears, the suffering, the wounding, and all that traps you in the past. You come to know that where you are now, exactly as you are now, is the perfect vehicle for Divine Intelligence. In truth, this is the only understanding and experience that allows you to be at peace.

Where you are now, exactly as you are now, is the perfect vehicle for Divine Intelligence.

Universal consciousness does not make mistakes. It has not created an imperfect being. It has created exactly what is needed to expand love, peace, fulfillment, and joy in this world. It uses your peculiarities, your differences, your idiosyncrasies, your perceived flaws, and even your subpersonalities to translate infinity into form. Feel that. Own it.

What stops you from seeing the perfection that exists is a combination of judgment and conditioning. But if you are connected to your Essential Self, doing what you are meant to be doing, you will never quite "fit in." That is because, in the exquisite majesty of your authenticity, you are as "bespoke" as they come. People will either hate you or love you for it, but that is irrelevant.

If you've ever gone to a fine-dining restaurant, you may notice that you either really like or really dislike your meal. Rarely is there an in-between. It's not like grabbing something at a fast-food chain, which would be described for the most part as convenient but not great. You, in your full glory, are a perfectly crafted dish, with the freshest organic ingredients, made by the world's best chef—a delicate risotto with English peas, a decadent lobster bisque, a tangy fennel and arugula salad, a succulent filet mignon, a rich chocolate mousse with a raspberry coulis. Your flavors and textures will resonate with some people, but not with others. It doesn't matter. What matters is that you stop trying to be a fast-food burger with a side of fries. Embrace yourself in your unique deliciousness. Be the best version of whatever dish you are. Live from the heart.

As St. Catherine of Siena put it, "Be who God meant you to be, and you will set the world on fire."

13

Harmony

WHAT DOES IT MEAN TO BE HUMAN? HOW DO we define ourselves as a species? What is our legacy?

One could reasonably argue that history is basically defined by wars. American history is defined by the Revolutionary War, the Civil War, World War I, World War II, the Cold War, the Korean and Vietnam Wars, and the wars in Iraq and Afghanistan. World history is defined by the rise and fall of empires, their ascendancy and their inevitable defeat. It is not really a pretty picture. But alongside all of the tumult, destruction, and bloodshed, there is literature, art, science, and philosophy. There are social compacts and sweeping reforms. There are the immortal plays of William Shakespeare; the dynamic paintings of Pablo Picasso; Jonas Salk's discovery and development of the polio vaccine; the enduring ideas of Plato, Aristotle, and Spinoza. There is the American Constitution and the civil rights movement. So many discoveries. So much creativity. There is influence, inspiration, expansion, beauty, and strength.

And yet, if you zoom in on people's lives, the way they interact throughout a day, you find that individuals are still wrestling with their internal struggles, their chattering minds, and their emotional turmoil. Young, old, male, female, adults, and children alike have made and continue to make their way through this earthly existence burdened with aching hearts, scattered minds, anger, reactivity, and hatred. Sometimes the outer circumstances are better, sometimes worse. Sometimes the struggle is for food and sometimes there is plenty, but seldom is there a sense of lasting internal fulfillment, peace, and love.

But all of that is changing. We are entering the Era

of the Soul, an age in which people will connect with and live life from their Essential Selves. In this emerging paradigm, what it means to be human is being redefined. People are hungry for a deeper understanding of who they really are; they want to awaken and know the Essential Self.

> *People are hungry for a deeper understanding of who they really are; they want to awaken and know the Essential Self.*

Awakening and knowing the Essential Self is a vibrational journey, and so forging ahead in this brave new world requires seeing yourself anew, from a vibrational standpoint. This process facilitates a vibrational realignment from fear to divine love, from struggle to universal freedom, from survival to complete abundance, and from resistance to merging into the flow of expansion and evolution, acceptance and flexibility. It moves us from experiencing inner restrictions, density, and limited states of consciousness to oneness, becoming one with everything. It is a movement from dissonance to complete resonance with the Divine, from nonalignment to complete alignment. It is a journey from insufficiency to fullness, from limits to expansion. And it is the journey from forgetting and veiling, obscuring your Essential Self, to complete remembrance and complete illumination.

Defining humanity as fearful, struggling, addicted, and weak is limited and incomplete. Defining humanity as the light of the Divine, as the Essential Self that is one with the one creative universal intelligence is expansive and complete.

Another concept from Hindu philosophy is important in understanding the redefinition of what it means to be human—the concept of the gunas. The gunas are three primary frequencies that describe your energy state at any given moment. *All three exist within you at all times, but the important thing is which is dominating, and this is always in flux.* The three gunas are *sattva*, harmony and purity; *rajas*, dynamism, activity, and self-centeredness; and *tamas*, negativity, dullness, fear, and disorder.

The Bhagavad Gita provides deep insight on how these three aspects present themselves in the individual: "Action that is virtuous, thought through, free from attachment, and without craving for results is considered

Sattvic; action that is driven purely by craving for pleasure, selfishness, and much effort is Rajasic; action that is undertaken because of delusion, disregarding consequences, without considering loss or injury to others or self is called Tamasic" (18:23–25).

Most of the world today is dominated by either *rajas* or *tamas*. *Rajas* is the raw ambition, the drive for pleasure, prestige, and position. It is the egoic fire. *Tamas* is different. It is heavy and slow. It is the thick fog of illusion that obscures truth. When the tamasic energy is strong in an individual, there is little self-awareness and an absence of higher consciousness resulting in reactivity. *Rajas* and *tamas* are by-products of separation and are held in place by your core wounding.

Your storehouse of samskaras creates the general vibrational state that you meet life with every day. As you raise your overall vibrational frequency through vibrational transformation, you are more likely to spend time in *sattva*. *Sattva*, the highest vibrational frequency, is the clean, pure vibration that is harmonic with your Essential Self. It supports everything in creation. When *sattva* is strong within you, you are drawn to eating habits that are more natural and organic and behaviors that enhance life. You do not feel drawn to foods and behaviors that denigrate your body. You are pulled into higher understandings and feel nonaligned with violence and fear. You feel compassion and love and express them naturally. Your energy attracts and draws toward itself all that supports soul connection.

My cat is always in harmony. He's sattvic when he's eating, killing a mouse, mating, peeing, sleeping, and even vomiting a hairball. That's because he's always fully aligned with his "catness"—his true, authentic, essential nature. All of nature is dominated by harmony, because plants and animals are always connected to who they are. To my knowledge, my cat has never thought he was worthless or felt shame or guilt. I have to admit I have superimposed my ideas on him a few times and thought he looked guilty when he overshot the litter box and peed on the floor, but that's my perception—not his. All of nature is always sattvic. Humans are the ones that alternate between dominating energies—*sattva*, *rajas*, *tamas*—not the rest of nature. A tree is always being a tree, fully, authentically, harmoniously. It never plays the role of an ant or a bird. It's never anything other than its Essential Self.

Harmony is authenticity. It is the essential nature of everything. You may think authenticity means perfectly playing the role you have chosen: being the perfect husband or wife, the best or smartest kid, or the most spiritual person. But though we tend to think of authenticity as the best performance, it's actually the opposite. True authenticity is being in harmony with your essential nature—regardless of circumstances. Just like my cat.

> *Harmony is authenticity. It is the essential nature of everything.*

When you feel dissonance, that is an invitation to return to harmony. Dissonance is a vibrational experience that is egoically based. Harmony and peace are vibrational experiences that exist on the level of the soul. When you are at peace, you are aligned with the soul. Everything else is ego.

> *When you are at peace, you are aligned with the soul. Everything else is ego.*

Being is a difficult concept for most people. Because we relate to the world on the level of the senses, we tend to favor tangibility and solidity. Being is about as far away from that as possible. You can't see it, smell it, taste it, hear it, or touch it. Being is beyond the emotions, the mind, and the body, but they all arise from it. Being is the silent ocean of awareness and the source of the active wave.

Your Essential Self, pure Being, is what harmonizes life. It is the foundation that stabilizes everything else. It is always there, but so often obscured and forgotten. When it's consciously present, consciously remembered and experienced, then you have restored wholeness and connection. Then you have redefined what it means to be human, and you have returned to harmony.

Imagine if the angst from your feelings of separation, resistance, and worthlessness evaporated. Imagine if what was left was oneness, peace, fulfillment, and love—a life in which you thrived. That is the promise of authenticity, of knowing your Essential Self. That is what harmony brings. It aligns you with your unique destiny and powers its spontaneous unfolding.

You will always play a role. It's part of your expression. Authenticity does not mean giving up your role. I will play the roles of husband, father, son, provider, author, and speaker. I will look and act certain ways. You will always play your roles and look and act certain ways.

And those roles will always be changing and morphing into more expanded versions of themselves.

But harmony arises when you realize that the role is not the whole story of *you*. Harmony arises when you reconnect with, remember, and realize the bigger part of you that was forgotten and hidden. This is the ultimate alignment: the role with the Essential Self. This is the restoration of oneness.

> *Harmony arises when you realize that the role is not the whole story of you.*

The redefinition of what it means to be human is a vibrational redefinition. It's a redefinition that moves from "dullness and fear" (*tamas*) to "doing" (*rajas*) and finally to "being" (*sattva*). It's a redefinition that moves from the human to the union of human and the Divine. It's not getting rid of the human. It's an all-inclusive redefinition that is both mortal and immortal—wave and ocean. You are more than your thoughts and feelings and body. You are more than your created self. You are universal consciousness.

The redefinition of what it means to be human is a vibrational redefinition that moves from "dullness and fear" (tamas) to "doing" (rajas) and finally to "being" (sattva).

No wonder the definition of what it means to be human has been so bleak and outwardly focused—the foundation and source have been forgotten. Being human is not just feelings, mind, and body. It is Essential Self, feelings, mind, and body. But you've forgotten the Divine Intelligence, the Observer, the Witness. That is your foundation. That is your realization. Being human is not just feeling, thinking, and acting. It is also Being. Consciously integrating Being—pure awareness, pure consciousness, the Essential Self—with feeling, thinking, and acting creates the fullness required for a connected, peaceful, and powerful life.

Knowing samadhi should not remain in the realm of possibility. It needs to move into the realm of lived reality. It is the final frontier for humanity.

This brings us to your expression of the Essential Self. How you express yourself in the world is actually a simple discussion. As we have said, life directly reflects your general vibrational frequency. Your general vibrational frequency determines your state of consciousness, the depth of connection to the Essential Self. That connection and state also determine the power and intelligence to which you have access. When your vibration is aligned and resonant with the highest and subtlest frequencies, then the Essential Self is accessible.

When you feel depressed, lost, fearful, and disconnected, you feel powerless, tired, and stressed, and nothing seems to go right. When you feel happy, centered, and connected, you feel powerful, energetic, and clear, and possibilities easily become reality.

When you are in vibrational alignment, your life spontaneously, naturally, and completely expresses the full intelligence and power of the Divine and becomes the vehicle for the Divine to express itself in the world through you. That creative intelligence is who you are now. Vibrational transformation is about realizing your already present Essential Self. It is not about turning you into someone different. When you know your Essential Self, you are fully the Divine expressing itself in this world. You express the attributes of peace, love, bliss, and abundance.

Redefining what it means to be human is an expansion of what is possible. You are not stuck in scarcity, limitation, suffering, or worthlessness. You turn from being solely outwardly focused to being outwardly *and* inwardly focused. You shift from fixating on feelings, thoughts, and action to embracing Being, feeling, thoughts, and action. You become the conscious experience of the Essential Self in the outer expression of life.

Being is divine; you are a human Being. Your intelligence, your wisdom, your power, your love, your confusion, your anger, your stress, your worthlessness—*all of it is divine.* Your redefinition of what it means to be human—your redefinition of self—requires that you love and accept it all: the enlightened part, the crazy part, the compassionate part, the loving, fearful, angry, and shameful parts.

It is all God knowing God.

14

The Five Commitments

ANYONE WHO HAS "MADE IT" CAN TELL YOU that success does not arrive serendipitously. It doesn't just happen. It is the result of years, sometimes decades of focus. Even when someone looks like an overnight success, there are years of effort, rejection, and persistence behind the moment of breakthrough. There is dedication, and there is devotion, but most of all there is commitment. People who do meet with success without having put in that kind of commitment often wind up breaking down in the limelight or losing it all, because they did not create a vessel to hold it in the first place.

In the same way, in order to live up to your potential, you need to commit to it. Commitment creates intention, and intention makes a desire worthy of manifestation. When you attribute worth to something, you elevate it and give it priority.

When you elevate and prioritize a goal or desire, you dedicate your intelligence and power to it. And when you bring your intelligence and power to bear on a goal, it comes into being.

> *Commitment creates intention, and intention makes a desire worthy of manifestation.*

I offer you the following five commitments. Allow them to become the foundation that powers your expansion. Moment by moment, day by day, month by month, let them guide your authenticity, your remembrance, your restoration, and your enlightenment into Being.

#1: Commit to Knowing Your Essential Self

You are walking around with a sort of amnesia. That is the effect of living in a created self. This is not an accident, nor is it wrong; the illusion of separation sets the stage for remembering oneness. The concealment allows for the revelation of your Essential Self by providing the perfect environment and structure you need to come into full remembrance.

I have discussed how you identify as the body, mind, and emotions. But the layers of identification are almost unlimited. Think about your concepts and beliefs. I am an American, and Russians are bad, or the other way around. I am a Republican, and Democrats will destroy the moral fabric of America, or the other way around. I am a Catholic, and I have the only true religion. I am straight, and gays are going to hell, or I am gay, and the straights are narrow-minded. So many beliefs and conditionings. So many layers of identification. And each layer creates fear, because it disconnects you from your Essential Self. Each layer covers over and shrouds your authenticity. Each layer separates you from what is true and loving.

You end separation and restore wholeness through the remembrance and revelation of the Essential Self, which is in union with the Divine. No two human beings achieve this revelation, this freedom, in the same way.

People think that imitation is the key to success. "If I do what that person did, if I follow these rules or this path, then I will arrive where I need to be." But the reality is that each individual is like a string on a musical instrument that, when strummed, sounds out a unique tone, contributing to the greater symphony of the whole universe. Two entrepreneurs in the same industry with the same education will still have distinct pathways to success. Twins raised in the same household will each have their own life to live, according to their individual vibration. We can hold one another's hands as we journey in this life, but it is up to each of us to carve our way, to learn how to trust our Essential Self and our passage through life.

We can hold one another's hands as we journey in this life, but it is up to each of us to carve our way, to learn how to trust our Essential Self and our passage through life.

To that point, I am writing this book to support you in experiencing your highest and best awakening. The most intelligent form of guidance is to bring people back to the truth of who they are, which is one with God. As the Roman Stoic philosopher Marcus Aurelius once wrote: "Above and below, all around, the elements dance. But the movement of virtue is not there. It is found by diving into the heart and advancing by a path, happily and invisibly. Trust that Power which knows the way."

To commit to your Essential Self is to fully employ the power of Divine Intelligence in your life, letting go of the attachments and expectations that cloud its transmission. It is coming into complete acceptance of yourself. When you can fully embrace your life as it is, you are able to receive that Divine Intelligence and its power, which is responsible for nature in all of its majesty. You have to learn to embrace yourself at every stage of your development, understanding that every part of you, including your anxiety, your pain, your neuroses, your fear, and your rage, all serve a purpose, until they don't.

In truth, you are the Observer of this life. It is grace that is guiding the unfolding of your evolution. Grace powers revelation; grace reveals oneness and your life's purpose. It is grace that restores full remembrance of your Essential Self.

This discovery, this unfolding, this realization, and this revelation is your commitment.

#2: Commit to a New Past, Present, and Future

When you live in a created self, you live in a world of false identifications, definitions, and beliefs. This colors how you see your life and how you see your past, present, and future. These misperceptions can be dramatic and add exponentially to your suffering.

You define your past by what has happened to you, by who did what to you, by how you were treated, loved, or abused. You define yourself by your experiences and by what was spoken over you or about you. You have taken all of that and personalized it by believing it is the truth of who you are. You hold firmly to the belief that the world did things to you. The result is a strong sense of victimhood. My parents abused me. My teachers belittled me. My ex-husband was mean and disrespectful to me. My business partner cheated me. The created self remembers a past of victimhood, generated by a limited vision, under a false judgment, in a sea of misperceptions. None of it is authentic or true, because life is never happening to you. It can only, in every case, be happening for you, for your expansion, for your evolution, for your awakening.

> *Life is never happening to you. It can only,*
> *in every case, be happening for you,*
> *for your expansion, for your evolution,*
> *for your awakening.*

Every person and every situation in your life is happening for you to remember who you authentically are, to remember your Essential Self. There is nothing extraneous, nothing superficial, nothing unconnected in your life. It's all happening for you, for remembrance. This is what grace is. This is what your past is. To embrace this truth is your commitment.

In the present, you live in a belief of worthlessness, inadequacy, and limitation, because you see yourself as the created self. You live with the subtle knowing that something isn't quite right, isn't quite true. And, for the most part, you don't have the time or inclination to address it, because you're too busy with work, family, and distractions. In your present reality, there is no present moment available to you. You have trained yourself out of experiencing the present. It is only in a state of connection, a state of awareness, a state of mindfulness that you can experience the present.

You are so convinced that the created self is who you are. On some level you know this created self is only a small part of the picture, but examining this would mean confronting your sense of unworthiness, your shame and fear. It's natural to avoid discomfort. And there is a lot of sadness in you. So you grasp at distraction and push away what you need to feel and look at. Instead you drink, smoke, do drugs, gamble, overeat, work incessantly, or lose yourself online in pornography or social media. It's a successful strategy for numbing, but it perpetuates suffering.

The present moment is the doorway to your magnificence and your limitless possibilities. It is the entry point to the soul. Loving "what is" in the present allows you to be open to receive all the possibilities of "more" that life wants to give you. What you love liberates, expands, and elevates you. What you resist imprisons you. What you fear condemns you. When you think life is a condition you have to overcome, change, or mold into shape, you cut yourself off from the fundamental reality, which is love, expansion, evolution, and light.

When you think life should be different than it is, you create a stream of invalidations, cutting off possibilities and maintaining powerlessness. The ability to shine the light of awareness on your internal landscape and bring resolution exists only in the present moment. Becoming consciously aware is a present-moment experience. Reality is only present-moment awareness. And above all else authenticity is accessed only in the present moment. Your real power exists in your ability to raise your vibrational frequency, to expand your consciousness, and to remember who you are. It is a commitment, instance by instance, acceptance by acceptance, allowance by allowance, to step into your power, harmony, and authenticity. This is your commitment to now.

> *Your real power exists in your ability to raise your vibrational frequency, to expand your consciousness, and to remember who you are.*

Your mind creates the vision of your future. At least your past comprises experiences around which you molded a false perception, but the future is imagined.

And of course it will be populated by everything that is inside you, all of your fears, beliefs, concepts, and identifications. Your future can become a fantasy nightmare created by false expectations; molded by unworthiness, inadequacy, and scarcity; driven by an unaligned attitude and approach; and residing in an environment of powerlessness.

Have your desires, but surrender your attachment to an outcome. Attachment to outcomes is your future framed with limitations and requirements. Attachment to outcomes limits possibilities and causes suffering. The future, in reality, holds possibilities beyond your ability to imagine. Life is always expanding into more. It is the law of the universe, so it is impossible for your future to be less expansive and evolved. It will be more, in all ways, for your benefit.

> *The future, in reality, holds possibilities beyond your ability to imagine.*

To see your past, present, and future in a new way is your commitment.

#3: Commit to Inner Peace

When the Essential Self is covered over, there is a contraction of energy that causes three things to happen. First, you feel imperfect and experience worthlessness. Second, you feel separate and experience duality. Third, you become caught up in the fruits of your actions and experience attachment to outcomes. These three together comprise the state that most people on this planet live in. The effect of this combination is fear, and fear causes you to live in reactive resistance to life. Fear, resistance, attachment, and control impede the flow of life, and thus your expansion and your evolution.

Resistance expresses itself as dissatisfaction with "what is." It is the opposite of acceptance and allowing. If you have $1,000, you want $10,000. If you are forty, you long to be thirty. If you have a three-bedroom house, you want a four-bedroom house. If you are on a spiritual path, you want more experiences. You grasp at what you want but don't have, and you push away what you have but don't want. You resist life, and in resisting life you suffer, living in a constant state of mental, emotional, and vibrational dissatisfaction, eliminating any possibility for peace, happiness, and fulfillment. Fear and resistance put you at war with your life.

You want to control life, meticulously molding it until it looks like your vision of what is best. You constantly fear that life will unfold in a way that is wrong, unsuitable, or harmful. You don't really believe that nature is always moving into more. You may believe that what is right for you, what works for you, is right and works for everyone.

Fear, resistance, attachment, and control are the modus operandi of the created self. Whenever you find yourself in resistance to "what is," whenever you find yourself attached to an outcome or angry because someone didn't act the way you wanted, whenever you find yourself wanting to control a person or situation, know that it is your created self operating from a place of fear.

Mindfulness is slowing down and moving into present-moment awareness, without judgment. When you bring mindfulness to how you resist life, to how you become attached to outcomes, to how you control life, you create a space, an opening for the light of conscious awareness to shine on the fear. When light shines in the darkness, the darkness disappears. The darkness is not attacked, figured out, fixed, analyzed, or pushed away. It is simply brought into consciousness, and that light of consciousness allows for the resolution and integration

of darkness. When fear is brought into conscious awareness, it loses its power. This allows peace.

> *When you bring mindfulness to how you*
> *resist life, to how you become attached*
> *to outcomes, to how you control life,*
> *you create a space, an opening for*
> *the light of conscious awareness*
> *to shine on the fear.*

Peace is an absence of war. That means your peace
arises when you stop your war with life, when you end
your resistance and opposition, when you move into allowing and acceptance. Peace is a state of tranquility,
without strife. That means you redefine your beliefs and
concepts as egoic points of view and align with what is
authentic and true.

One who embodies peace becomes a catalyst for
peace in the world. Peace isn't something you create as
much as it is an effect of alignment, allowing, and resonance. When the battle with life ceases, when the resistance to life subsides, when you let go of control and

begin to surrender, when you let go of attachment, you are left with peace. Commit to your peace.

#4: Commit to Fulfillment

Fulfillment means different things to different people. To a spiritual person, it could mean enlightenment. To your trainer at the gym, it could mean a perfect body. To a material person, it could mean wealth and power. To an up-and-coming chef, it could mean financial backing to open a restaurant. To a college professor, it could mean knowing everything about her chosen field. True fulfillment arises when you perform your duty, when you finish what you set out to accomplish, when you move in the direction of your purpose. Your purpose is to know your Essential Self and fully express that in the world. That simple sentence encompasses both the spiritual and the material. It is about enlightenment, material success, and happiness. It also includes the concept of thriving. Thriving and fulfillment are inexorably linked.

Thriving means to prosper and flourish. You have a body, a mind, emotions, and a spirit. Think about what it means to prosper and flourish, to really thrive, on all levels. For your body to thrive it must be accomplishing its purpose. You might automatically think that means perfect health. But in actuality that means it is both serving as the vehicle for expression of your Essential Self and perfectly supporting your journey to self-knowledge. It is your body playing its role in your life's purpose.

The same goes for your mind. Your mind has a role to play. It identifies, analyzes, makes determinations, and relates to the outside world. It also is a vehicle through which you express and know your life's purpose. It has its role in expressing creativity and expansion and in knowing your Essential Self. When your mind is thriving, it is functioning in support of your life's purpose.

Your feelings are like a very refined thermometer that measures alignment of vibrational frequencies. A non-aligned vibration will feel bad, and an aligned vibration will feel good. You make your decisions based upon this criterion more than you realize. You can intellectually analyze something all day and it may sound perfect, but if it doesn't feel good, you won't go for it. Your feelings also play a significant role in defining and expressing your purpose.

In society, fulfillment is sometimes linked directly to success. Success is linked to money, power, relationships, and position. But you know what happens: the famous young singer who shot to stardom has a meltdown, the perfect couple gets divorced, and the person who was promoted to vice president gets fired. Success is more than the achievement. Success must include thriving: a quiet mind, more time to spend with family or in nature, moving toward your purpose in life.

Life has its inner and outer reality, and fulfillment is both internal and external. It is critical that you have 200 percent fulfillment: 100 percent inner fulfillment and 100 percent outer fulfillment. Inner fulfillment is about knowing your Essential Self, and outer fulfillment is about supporting your body, mind, and emotions, so they can do their part in expressing your unique contribution in the world. Living 200 percent of life is your commitment. Fulfillment is your commitment.

#5: Commit to Unlimited Possibilities

When you live in inadequacy, limitation, unworthiness, or fear, you create a relationship with them. Imagine being married to unworthiness. It isn't who you are, but it follows you everywhere. It lives with you 24/7. It talks to you regularly. It takes a lot of care, time, and energy. And most important, this relationship defines you and what is possible in your life. It's a very one-sided relationship, because it offers you nothing and requires almost everything.

When you define yourself as unworthy, you create an energy barrier to receiving all that is meant for you. It's difficult to leap from believing you are unworthy to believing you are deserving, but you can move slowly in the right direction by redefining yourself. It can't be just words or wishful thinking. Moving toward self-love requires a rise in vibrational frequency—a vibrational leap, an upleveling.

Trust supports making these vibrational leaps. Trust allows flow, and flow opens you to possibility. The trust I am talking about is knowing the universe is unfolding for your expansion and unfolding the realization of your divinity. So if you want to redefine what is possible in your life, you begin with accepting and trusting what is true and authentic. Trust opens you to receive, and the foundation of trust is acceptance.

Trust allows flow,
and flow opens you to possibility.

You are a unique expression of the Divine, and so you will have unique qualities. How you are uniquely expressing now is the perfect place for you, the perfect way for you to be, the perfect point to move into more expansion and evolution. This is your jumping-off point into more. There is nothing wrong with you, nothing that needs to be fixed. All you need is acceptance. There is no mistake that you are who, what, and where you are. You are perfect as you are.

The law of the universe is that everything is always moving into more expansion and evolution. That is the only possibility that is real and authentic for you. There is no other possibility. You can only accept that you are moving into more.

Here's the catch. You have defined what that "more" looks like. It can only look the way you have believed it should be. If you are poor, more means rich. If you are unworthy, more is acceptance by others. If you are sick, more means health. But the universe has your destiny, your remembrance and realization laid out in a perfect road map that most probably doesn't look anything like your road map. So when life shows up and it doesn't look like what you have defined as "more," you reject and resist it. You refuse to look at it and identify the opportunity and the possibilities contained within the new situation.

Here's where trust comes in. Whatever is showing up is the perfect "more" for you. You can believe that because that is the only way the universe acts. What you need to do is use your awareness, your mindfulness, and your ability to see deeply to look at and identify what that more is. This is how you recognize possibility. This is how unlimited possibilities unfold. They are always showing up, but they remain inert and are passed over unless you recognize their existence and seize the opportunity.

Whatever is showing up
is the perfect "more" for you.

When you start to consciously recognize that the universe is continually delivering you expansive and new possibilities at every turn, then you can trust and believe that unlimited possibilities exist and are, in fact, consistently presenting themselves to you. Then potential can be recognized and become reality. Limitless possibilities becoming your reality is your commitment.

15

Trust and Surrender

ONCE YOU END YOUR RESISTANCE AND MOVE into acceptance and allowing, once you become aware of the infinite potential that resides beyond your five senses, and once you prioritize living the five commitments, the final doorways to knowing your Essential Self are trust and surrender. Only in a state of complete trust, with the energies of fear and survival resolved, can you fully receive the blessings and opportunities that are available to you.

How many times have you heard the story of the person who finds the career of his dreams once he let go of a mediocre job that wasn't allowing his quirky creativity to show? Or what about that person who finally dared to leave a long-term but stifling relationship, only to wind up meeting her soul mate soon after? How many people do you know who finally let go of their victimhood, only to be met with incredible empowerment? And what about those people who just seem to be in the right place at the right time? There they are, going about their business, picking out apples at Whole Foods, when they meet their next business partner, or spiritual teacher, or husband or wife.

This is what happens when you choose to let go, to surrender and trust the flow to carry you, even if you don't exactly know where. You wind up in scenarios that sparkle with synchronicity; your life expands as it resonates with your soul. No matter where you are, you feel at home, because that feeling of home is the Divine within you.

No matter where you are, you feel at home, because that feeling of home is the Divine within you.

When you are in a state of trust and surrender, you are acknowledging that there is an organizing principle taking care of you. You are accepting the truth that reality is on your side. You are defining your human experience as one in which all that you need will come to you. The more you relax into that receiving, the faster it shows up as a physical manifestation in reality.

Surrender allows you to relinquish your personal will and align with Divine will. What your personality determines is best evaporates. You are no longer limiting your possibilities. Grace steers the bus.

Trust naturally arises from within through the gradual surrendering of your individual wants. Trust is the spontaneous alignment with "what is," and through that trust there is samadhi. Samadhi is the complete embracing of reality, as it is. There is no difference between the inner and outer experience. They become one.

> *Trust is the spontaneous alignment with "what is," and through that trust there is samadhi.*

There are already things you do not question in life, of course; there are aspects of your life that are already fully aligned. You don't question if the sun will rise or if day will follow night. You don't question if you are going to exhale once you've inhaled. Feel the trust of those aspects of your life—and then transfer them to the areas where you don't feel so sure. Use them to your advantage.

Imagine trust and surrender as the pure white dove with the fresh olive sprig in its mouth: it is the assurance of your restoration, as if it has all already come to pass. Trust is acknowledging the perfection of your destiny and the joy and wonderment at its unfolding. Conscious awareness, expanded mindfulness, acceptance, alignment, and harmony are all part of the greater awakening that tells you it's okay to release your grip. Trust and surrender are whispering to you that you can end your suffering and find peace.

Trust and surrender are whispering to you that you can end your suffering and find peace.

As a human being, you often feel the aspiration to do something extraordinary with your life. The trait you wish to have—the prowess of a world-renowned athlete, the strength of a world leader, or the artistic talent of a famous painter—is born from a willingness to let go and align yourself with the Divine. You have the same raw fundamental potential—not born of your circumstances, location, and bank account—but born of the soul. Your greatness is directly derived and accessed through your willingness to open yourself up to your divine glory and to live in trust and connection to that source.

Maybe you cannot leap all at once. Maybe, for now, you slightly lessen your grip on control and find a little peace. For now, it is enough to make only a few shifts, to take one step outside your comfort zone and relax. Breathe. Explore within. The world outside you will unfold and take care of itself. For today, you can take that one step, that small vibrational leap. As you do this, little by little, acceptance by acceptance, you will start to feel lighter. The heavy energy of resistance will lighten, and the fear will recede, one vibrational change at a time.

When you live in a created self, life is seen as happening to you. When you step onto the path of resolution, transformation, and integration, you see life happening for you. That allows you to start to surrender, because you begin to see the hand of divine grace at work in your life. It is in that surrender that acceptance reaches its fulfillment. Life will always accurately mirror your internal state of being. When you are contracted, heavy with vibrational density, and resisting life, the challenges of life are numerous and overwhelming. As you reclaim your Essential Self, the greatest transformation of all reveals itself. Life isn't just happening for you; life reflects *as you*.

In that expanded state, the individual drop of water merges with the ocean. Oneness becomes possible. Boundaries and differences evaporate. Complete trust emerges as the realization dawns that there is only one consciousness, only one energy. There is only the Divine, who became you, concealed its divinity for a while but now is fully revealed.

Somewhere along the way, surrender will begin to reveal itself. Eventually, you will wake up one day and say, "Wow, I took one step every day, and now I have arrived at an amazing place. That was a journey worth taking. The heaviness is lighter, the suffering is gone, the resistance has eased, the fear is dissolved, and life is happening for me." Life will flow easily, and struggle will end. And most of all you will discover *you*. You will remember your true Essential Self and know your wholeness, your divinity, your blessedness. Eventually, you will experience a new reality, life happening as you—connection—samadhi.

Life, you, me, the cat, the anger, the fear, the adulation, the grief, the hope, and the samadhi are all one. They are the play of consciousness, the great emergence and remembrance. They are all part of your return home, your return to wholeness, your recognition. They are love merging into love, the river of love merging into the ocean of love.

In the end, life is but the light of the Divine merging into the light of the Divine.

That is what remembrance, recognition, illumination, enlightenment, self-realization, and samadhi are. It is my heart and your heart merging with God's heart, because there is only one heart anyway. There is only one awareness, one consciousness, one energy, one love. There are only blessings. There is only grace.

ACKNOWLEDGMENTS

Everything originates from love. It would be impossible for me to be able to thank everyone who has played a part in bringing this book into being. That list would consist of all the individuals who have played their part perfectly in helping me to finally get to a place of freedom from which I am now able to express my evolutionary potential. In truth this book was created long before I had the courage to consciously accept my role as a messenger. I am grateful for every loving embrace, each piece of guidance, and the totality of the love that has led me to this moment, as I now recognize and embrace it all as God.

I do wish to consciously acknowledge those who have directly impacted my ability to bring forth this book. Thanks go to:

My entire team at the Desai Companies, for your

patience, dedication, and tireless commitment to this work and the global community you support.

My amazing agent, Amanda Annis, and the entire team at Trident Media for holding the highest expectation for this expression.

Gideon Weil and the whole HarperOne family for the loving and supportive way that you have embraced me and nurtured my voice as an instrument for global transformation.

My dear friend James Pesavento, for your loving guidance, support, and unwavering devotion to the elimination of suffering for all.

And finally to you, the reader. Thank you for answering the call to live your limitless potential. May this book serve as the starting point of a deeper journey of remembrance, one that guides you back to the fullness of your Essential Nature.

ABOUT THE AUTHOR

Panache Desai is a bestselling author, thought leader, and life catalyst whose loving, compassionate presence and unique power of insight have transformed countless individuals, organizations, and companies. Through energetic transformation, Panache helps people break free from suffering and limitation on every level, fostering a deeper understanding of who they are, and guiding them into greater states of connection, collaboration, and love.